T0171471

BARACK

★ ★ ★ Like Me ★ ★ ★

The Chocolate-Covered Truth

DAVID ALAN GRIER

with Alan Eisenstock

A TOUCHSTONE BOOK

Published by Simon & Schuster

New York   London   Toronto   Sydney

Touchstone
A Division of Simon & Schuster, Inc.
1230 Avenue of the Americas
New York, NY 10020

First Touchstone hardcover edition October 2009

TOUCHSTONE and colophon are registered trademarks of Simon & Schuster, Inc.

For information about special discounts for bulk purchases,
please contact Simon & Schuster Special Sales at
1-866-506-1949 or business@simonandschuster.com.

The Simon & Schuster Speakers Bureau can bring authors to your live event.
For more information or to book an event, contact the Simon & Schuster Speakers
Bureau at 1-866-248-3049 or visit our website at www.simonspeakers.com.

Designed by Joy O'Meara

Manufactured in the United States of America

1   3   5   7   9   10   8   6   4   2

Library of Congress Cataloging-in-Publication Data
Grier, David Alan
Barack like me : the chocolate covered truth / David Alan Grier with Alan Eisenstock.
p.   cm.
"A Touchstone book."
1. Grier, David Alan, 1955 June 30–   2. African American comedians—Biography.
3. Grier, David Alan, 1955 June 30– —Political and social views.   4. United States—
Race relations—Political aspects.   5. United States—Social conditions—21st century.
6. African Americans—Race identity—Political aspects.   7. African Americans—
Social conditions—21st century.   I. Eisenstock, Alan.   II. Title.
PN2287.G695A3 2009
792.702'8092—dc22
[B]
2009018703

ISBN   978-1-4391-5682-7

To the love of my life,
my darling daughter Lulu

CONTENTS

Contents

Contents

✶ ✶ ✶ PREFACE ✶ ✶ ✶

Ray Charles said the secret to life is *timing*. He was right on, especially when it comes to writing a book. When I handed in this book back in April 2009, Barack Obama was riding high and I was a happily married man.

Now it's more than six months later. Barack's approval ratings have fallen and so have mine.

Sadly, my wife and I are in the process of divorcing. Everything I wrote in *Barack Like Me* happened. Everything I said and felt was the truth . . . at the time. I am amazed at how life constantly hits you with surprises, changes, and challenges. I'm even more amazed at our ability to survive and bounce back.

Enjoy my book. It's real!

BARACK
✷ ✷ ✷ **Like Me** ✷ ✷ ✷

✴ ✴ ✴ **1** ✴ ✴ ✴

SECRETARY OF MIRTH

Yes, we can!

And yes, we did.

We won!

January 2009. Going on two and a half months now and they haven't taken it back.

I still don't trust it. Every morning when I wake up I check and double-check. I need confirmation.

First thing I do is blink a couple of times to make sure I'm not dreaming. I lean over and kiss my wife, Christine, kiss and nuzzle my daughter, Luisa, check myself, see if I'm alive, yep, got all my parts, turn on CNN and NPR at the same time, even flip to Fox News, and yes—confirm—it's still true.

Barack Obama is president of the United States.

It really happened.

Elected in a landslide, too. Over 69 million people voted for him, poked that chad, popped that cherry. Sixty-nine million people.

Incredible. Amazing. Historic.

True.

And here we are, Christine and I, invited guests to the Purple Ball on Inauguration Day, slammed up against the stage in this hangar-sized ballroom, purple neon strobe light stabbing our eyes, a throng of people mashed up against us, waiting for President Barack Obama and First Lady Michelle to arrive.

I admit it. I am in awe of this man. Today he will speak and dance at ten inaugural balls. *Ten.* Tomorrow he'll be up at 5:00 a.m. to start his presidency. He promises to hit the ground running. Are you serious? I wouldn't have gotten out of bed for three days.

A black president. Can you get your head around that? We've had black presidents before, but only on television and in the movies. And the moment a black guy becomes president, the world is about to end. Like in the movie *Deep Impact*, President Morgan Freeman doesn't merely inherit the worst economic crisis in a century. No. That would be too easy. He inherits an asteroid flying through space about to blow up the earth.

In the back of my mind, I worry that Barack Obama's presidency is doomed to fail. A young guy I spoke to on the street in New York said it best: "It's obviously a plot. It's rigged."

I keep hearing those words: it's rigged. Meaning that the only way that America elected a black man is because stuff is so fucked up, nobody can solve the problems. They put the brotha in to fail. And when he fails, they'll say, "See? We told you," and it's back to business as usual. We'll be lucky if a black guy gets elected president of the NAACP.

At the Purple Ball, my attention turns to a commotion from somewhere behind the stage. I hear urgent whispers and voices crackling through walkie-talkies, music suddenly blares, cranked up, and screaming, cheering, and applause from the hundreds of people behind me pound me like a thunderclap, and I gasp, I literally gasp, a lump rises in my throat, and appearing through what seems like the blue light of a camera flash, Barack Obama, the president of the United States of America, *our* president, walks out from the wings, in the words of Stuart Scott on ESPN, as cool as the other side of the pillow, strolling hand in hand with the First Lady, Michelle Obama, who in person, I'm telling you, is so beautiful she weakens my knees.

They bow slightly, like royalty, and then they clap, for *us.* They are both smiling. Grinning, really. But these are not triumphant smiles. They are modest smiles, smiles of acceptance, smiles of thanks.

Barack wears a black tuxedo. He looks thin and fit, taller than you'd think, his hoop player's frame tucked into his tux sharp and taut. He would look cool in anything—tuxedo, sweat suit, bathrobe, toga, it wouldn't matter.

Now Michelle swirls toward us wearing this off-white, one-shoulder, chiffon-y gown created by a young designer named Jason Wu. She is beaming and clapping and then waving, and she is beyond magnificent. She is radiant. The kind of stunning we've seen only once before in a First Lady, that being Jackie Kennedy.

I want to cry, but, frankly, I'm cried out. My tears have been flowing freely over the last months, often at the most unexpected and, yes, embarrassing times. But today, at this moment, while I'm moved and the emotions rise up, I feel strong. And proud. No. That's not quite it. I feel more than proud. I feel—

Right.

Yes.

I feel that what is happening here, what I am witnessing, what I am experiencing is finally . . . right.

And I know that the journey I took to get here, the one ending at this inaugural ball, a journey that started before I was born, when my grandparents lived in the segregated South, a journey that took my family through backbreaking work in the fields, and riding in the back of the bus, is a journey that lives inside my soul. That's why this moment feels right.

His smile widening bright enough to light the entire ballroom, President Barack Obama waves his hand to quiet the crowd. Not going to happen. The crowd roars louder. He laughs, enjoying the love that rushes over him and Michelle like a wave. He dips his head, feeling a little humbled and clearly overwhelmed. He waves again, a parade wave, and opens his mouth to speak, laughs, tries to speak again, and then after maybe thirty seconds, except for a few scattered shouts of untamed joy, the crowd quiets.

"I want to thank all of you not merely for helping me get elected,"

Barack says. "But I want to thank each and every one of you for what you do to make this country special—"

Huge applause. Foot stomping. Howling.

"And I want to thank each and every one of you—"

Barack suddenly stops. All eyes are on him. Riveted.

"Oh, my God," he says. "DAG!"

He grins, cocks and loads a finger pistol, lowers it, takes aim, fires off one shot and—*bang!*—hits me right between the eyes. He laughs.

"Hey, DAG, I have to bring you up and say hi."

My wife's mouth opens and closes like a trapdoor.

"Come on up here," Barack says.

"No, no, Barack, it's cool, you're right in the middle of your speech—"

He waves me away. "This speech is nothing. Give DAG a hand, Michelle. Wait. Let's get Christine first."

With applause and cheering building at our backs, Barack and Michelle lean down and pull Christine up onto the stage, then guide me as I climb up next to her. I flash the victory sign to the crowd with both hands. Barack beams, shakes his head, and hugs me.

"We did it, man," he says.

"Yes, we did, Barack. I mean, Mr. President."

"Don't be like that now. All formal. You call me Barack. All the time."

He slaps my chest. I nod. Around us, music comes up, swells. A soaring violin intro to "At Last." Michelle smiles, sways, taps my wife on the shoulder.

"I'm sorry, Christine. Do you mind if I dance with your husband?"

"Not at all," Christine says.

"In that case, may I have this dance?" the president says, bowing to Christine, who curtsies.

I sweep Michelle into a simple box step. She's light on her feet, an accomplished dancer.

"I loved the *Chocolate News*," she says. "I always thought you were underrated. The industry takes you for granted."

"Thank you. That's very kind. I don't know if I'm taken for granted. Okay, maybe a little—"

"Well, we're big fans at our house," she says. "And of course the girls adore *Jumanji*. Their favorite scene is when you get crushed to death in that giant pod."

"That is so nice," I say. "I think."

Michelle laughs, then pulls back slightly. "Oh, DAG, before I forget and the night gets too crazy, let's exchange numbers. The girls are dying to babysit Lulu. They're very responsible. I made them take a babysitting course and CPR so they're certified."

The music hits a crescendo, and then, as if we've rehearsed, Barack and I twirl Christine and Michelle at exactly the same time. The crowd goes insane. We bow.

"We got to get over to the MTV Ball," Barack says to me as he links his hand into Michelle's. "You got my private number?"

"I think I do," I say.

"Call me," Barack says. "Or better, text me. The day gets long, I could use a laugh or just a hey."

"I will."

"I'm serious," Barack says.

"I got you," I say.

"God bless America!" Barack says, his hand and Michelle's entwined and clasped over his head, waving to the cheering crowd. He leads Michelle away. Turns. Points at me. Then they go.

*　*　*

I don't want to push it. Don't want to impose. I feel it's only fair to give Barack ample time to settle in.

I call him first thing next morning.

"Hey, what's up, Barack?"

"Hey, what's up, DAG?"

"You know. This, that. So what you doing, man?"

"Running the country, man. You know how we do. Passing bills, man, passing bills. Trying to get shit through, man."

"Yeah. I know they on you, man."

"Yeah. It's hardball, man. You know what it's like."

"I do."

"Hey, man, I got to go to a meeting. Let me get you back."

"Later."

Ten minutes later Christine and I hail a cab, head out to breakfast. A text comes in. Barack. Sending me a smiley face.

Barack is so cool.

*　*　*

An hour later I get the call I've been expecting.

"Hey, what's up, DAG?"

"Whadup, Barack?"

"I've been thinking. You should be in my Cabinet, man."

"Damn right I should be in your motherfucking Cabinet, man. About time you asked me, man."

"What you want to be? Secretary of what?"

"Secretary of Mirth."

Barack laughs. "I like it. I have to *create* a Cabinet position for you. Secretary of Mirth."

"My job will be spreading mirth throughout the globe."

"Invest in the new global hilarity," Barack says, and now we're both laughing. "I want to get this done today. I'm on it."

"Good. I want to get to work," I say.

"Quick question," Barack says, still chuckling.

"Shoot."

"Have you, by any chance, employed any illegal aliens?"

"I'm sure I have," I say, laughing. "We hired this woman a few years back? She couldn't speak English. She didn't have a car. I'm sure she was not correct. I'm positive she had no papers. Illegal as cocaine, dawg."

"You took care of that, right?"

"Hell, no. Barack, man, everybody I know in L.A. has illegal help. I mean, dude, *please.*"

The line goes dead.

"Hello? Barack? Don't hang up on me, man! I was playing! *Hello?* I'm the Secretary of Mirth! I WANT MY CABINET POSITION! HELLO??? *BARACK!!!*—"

"David!"

I blink through the mist that has descended over my eyes.

"Huh?"

"Wake up!"

After a minute of furious REM, I'm able to focus on a frightened flight attendant who's standing next to me, a cocktail napkin fluttering in her hand.

I sit up in my seat, make out Christine next to me.

"Do you want something to drink?" my wife asks softly, deliberately, as if I'm a child of five.

"Do I—want—no, thank you—yes . . . a . . . water, no, a juice . . . a water and a juice."

I smile at the flight attendant. She smiles back, fake, plastic, the kind of practiced smile she fastens in place when dealing with passengers who are crazy, obnoxious, or on their way to prison handcuffed to the cop next to them.

"Are you all right?" Christine whispers.

"I fell asleep," I say. "I had this crazy dream."

"Apparently," my wife says. "You were screaming that you wanted a Cabinet position."

I yawn, get my bearings, glance around the plane. Slowly, it all comes back to me. The insanity of that morning. Bundling up Luisa and bringing her to her grandmother's. Driving all night from San Francisco to Los Angeles. Packing our bags, showering, and changing in less than an hour. Running late for our flight, scrambling out of the cab, dashing into the terminal. Arriving at our gate and seeing that every single person on our flight is heading to the inauguration. More than half of the passengers are decked out in Obama gear— T-shirts, skirts, hats, pins, ribbons, Barack's face plastered all over, layered in red, white, and blue. People are snapping pictures of each other, even if they've just met. Christine and I join in, taking pictures and posing with total strangers who right now feel like family. We are rejoicing, all of us, documenting this momentous occasion, sharing this once-in-a-lifetime event, starting the party early. The plane, this Virgin Airlines direct flight to D.C., feels like a Las Vegas–bound spring break party bus. We are all basking in the excitement, in the anticipation. And, yes, symbolism, we're flying *Virgin* Airlines. Perfect. For we are all on the maiden voyage, the first flight, all of us, en route to celebrating our first black president.

✷ ✷ ✷ **2** ✷ ✷ ✷

BEIGE IS THE NEW BLACK

A few months ago, I saw this West Virginia coal miner, white guy, being interviewed on TV. Real redneck. I'm talking about a one-tooth, throwback hillbilly. He couldn't even pronounce "Barack Obama." But he said to the interviewer, "Look, man, I am voting for him. We need to make changes here. I will vote for a frog if it will help me feed my family."

I thought, *Man, we have come a long way. To him, it is beyond race. Barack Obama is just the best guy for president. He sees him only as someone who can help.*

I know that early on, when Barack started running, before the first primary, before the Iowa caucuses, we weren't there yet. He wasn't really clicking. A lot of people confused Barack Obama with the other guy, the guy whose name sounds like Obama. I heard people saying, dubiously, "That's the guy with the beard and the cave, and now he's running for president? This is a great country. Look at him. He's really cleaned up. Lost the beard. He looks like a nice guy. He's not so scary looking. He doesn't hate us anymore, huh? He wants to lead us. You have to love America."

Then people started to figure out who Barack Obama was, where he came from, and what he stood for. He spent most of his time and energy going on the road, talking to people, mostly white people, convincing them. "Hey, look, I'm not scary. I'm just like you. See, I have a wife. I have two kids. I'm not crazy. I don't have a tail."

Gradually, people got to know him and discovered that they liked him. He wasn't angry. He didn't come across like Al Sharpton or Jesse Jackson. He wasn't trying to stir things up. He looked okay, even presidential. He didn't look too "black." He didn't have dreadlocks. He didn't wear a hoodie. We know he smoked cigarettes, but Michelle made him stop. A point for him. Two points for her.

He seemed very comfortable and happy in his marriage. And so did she. They came across as a great couple, interesting, intelligent, funny, people you'd invite to dinner, have over for potluck, play charades.

But when the primaries began, it seemed that everyone had already conceded the nomination to Hillary Clinton. It was her time, her turn. She had a lock on the election. Except they didn't count on Barack Obama. They underestimated him. He surprised the world and won the Iowa caucuses, then he started winning primaries, and

Hillary started to panic. She came out fighting, flexed her muscles. Her campaign turned on a dime and went all hard-ass. It was all about, "See how accomplished Hillary is? She can arm-wrestle you. She can drink you under the table. If she punches you, she will knock you out. She has skills and you have shit."

Then her campaign flipped even more and turned ugly. She was so desperate to be president that she would try anything, any tactic. She tried everything but screaming rape. I wanted to call out Bill Clinton. I wanted to say to him, "If it's true that you were the first black president, then brotha, please . . . get your woman in check. She's running wild. Get control of your woman. What kind of black man are you?"

Barack never panicked, never lost his cool, and he kept winning. It got tight toward the end, but finally, kicking and screaming, Hillary dropped out, Barack got the nomination, and rolled in for the win. Hillary got her reward, too. Secretary of state. Big job. Lot of responsibility, and most important, a lot of travel. I know who put the thought in Barack's head: Bill. I know he whispered in his ear, "Barack, please, send her on the road so I can have the house to myself. Please. Get her out of the country. This weekend if possible. I got two sororities on call and a whole bunch of kegs just waiting for me to bust open."

* * *

My quick, hourly reality check.

Barack Obama is still president, right?

I have to ask. Because our economy is so bad, he could get laid off. Could happen. The brother is always the last hired and first fired. Our luck. We finally get a president and before his ass hits the chair, he gets a voice mail, "We need to see you in my office, right away."

"Hey, guys, what's up?"

"Listen, Mr. President, you're doing a great job, you really are, people are very impressed. This is awkward. We're gonna have to let you go."

"But I won the election."

"I know. Which makes it harder."

"Damn. Do I at least get two weeks' notice?"

"I'm sorry. Clean out your desk and hand over your keys. The guys here will escort you out of the building."

He'd slouch home in the middle of the day, looking grim and defeated, barely able to make eye contact with Michelle.

"You're home early, Barack."

"I got laid off."

"What? You're no longer president?"

"No. Ambassador. Pack everything up. Pull the kids out of school. We're moving to Afghanistan."

"Afghanistan? We're at war there!"

"Honey, in this economy, at least I got a job."

I know. Not gonna happen. He's cool. Truth is we're flying high. Being black like Barack is the new, new thing. Every pundit from Larry King to *Atlantic* magazine agrees: black is in. All shades of black. Which is good for most people, because so many of us are of mixed race. Myself included. It's mind-boggling that we have ended up here, at this point in our history. There was a time, only a few generations ago, that being of mixed race was not so cool. In fact, it was illegal to try to pass yourself off as a different race. If the authorities found out, you lost everything—your position, your home, and all your possessions. You'd be separated from your family and often lynched.

President Barack Obama has changed all that. People now want to be mixed. Bi-racial, tri-racial, quad- and quinti-racial, how many you got? The more the better. Multi-racial is the hot new facial, the best look in the book. Mixed race is the new superrace. If you look too black, people seem disappointed. They look at you and say, "You're just black. Oh. That's too bad. Are you sure? Anything else in there?"

They're looking for the Obama mix. It's like a new kind of coffee. "We just came up with it. Try this. The new Obama roast. It's the perfect blend. Strong, but not sharp. Seductive. Bold. Sweet. Smooth. And not too dark. Not like that Dikembe Mutombo roast they're brewing across the street."

And why not be black like Barack? He's the coolest guy on the planet right now. He's bigger than any rapper, more popular than any rock star. He's huge. We admire him and kids aspire to be like him.

Sometimes we even go too far.

I have a very close friend, who, when I first met him, told me that he was half Mexican. Not sure how that came up. He just made a point of telling me.

I shrugged and said, "All right, cool. Whatever." I'm wondering what half Mexican looks like, because his Mexican half is pretty well embedded. I never give it a second thought, but for some reason his being half Mexican comes up in almost every one of our conversations. One night, he and his wife invite me over for dinner. His wife is charming, smart, funny, and pretty much entirely Puerto Rican.

We're sitting around the dinner table, having a great time, laughing, chilling, and I say casually, just making small talk, "Well, you know with your husband being half Mexican and all—"

A plate falls out of his wife's hand. Flutters toward the real, genuine Mexican tile floor like a dying bird. I dive for it and snatch it out of the air before it smashes into a million pieces.

She is looking at him but talking to me. "He is half what?"

"Mexican," I say.

His wife now fixes my friend with a Jedi laser stare. "You are *what*?"

"Mexican?" he squeaks like a mouse.

His wife nods. "May I see you for a moment in the kitchen?"

"Now?"

"Immediately."

His wife blasts out of her chair as if shot by a cannon and storms out of the room with my friend trailing ten feet behind. The kitchen door flies open, then swings shut with a *bang*. A short, muffled, indecipherable "conversation" carries through the door, then the door flies open again and my friend and his wife—her head thrown back defiantly, my friend looking stricken and whiter than Liquid Paper— return to the dining room.

"We have an announcement to make," she says. She folds her hands under her chin and glares at her husband. He stares speechless into a bowl of rapidly browning guacamole, then finally speaks.

"Okay, see. I'm, okay, I'm not, well, you know, Mexican. Half. I'm not half Mexican. I'm not Mexican. At all."

"I am aware of that now," I say.

"I don't know why I said I was," my friend says miserably.

"It doesn't matter," I say.

"I've always wanted to be Mexican," he moans. "Ever since I was a little kid. I used to call myself Roberto."

I gently lay my hand on his shoulder.

He shakes his head. "You guys are all something else. You guys are all mixed. You're all great."

"Well, you're something, too," I say.

"I'm just white," he says. It sounds like a death sentence.

"If you want," I say, "I will call you Roberto."

"No," his wife says.

"You didn't let me finish," I say. "What I meant was." I swallow. "More wine? Anyone? I brought this good bottle of red. Let me pour. This is so good. Umm. I believe Parker rated this baby like a 127, blindfolded—"

✳ ✳ ✳

Barack is president. Black is in. Black is cool. Everyone wants to be black now. But Obama black. Tiger Woods black. Halle Berry black.

Not Samuel L. Jackson black. Or OJ black. Or Mike Tyson black.

I also think that having Barack as the leader of the free world gives us at least a temporary pass. Until he fucks up. But he'd have to fuck up worse than the last guy, and that just isn't possible. So I think we're all right for a while.

Still, I worry that it will all come tumbling down in the blink of an eye. It used to be, before Barack, that if I saw a piece on the news about a guy shooting up a 7-Eleven and killing twenty-seven people, I'd pray, "Please don't let this guy be black. We don't need that. Wait. There he is. He's coming out of the store with his hands up. He's . . . *Armenian*! All right! Thank God!"

As black has become, for now, the "in hue," that is, as long as Barack is cool and going strong, I'm amused at how popular culture—popular white culture—defines being black. As a kid, I remember seeing the movie *Black Like Me*. In this movie, a white guy's skin turns black and all of a sudden, he's saying, "Hey, Daddy-O, let's go hear some jazz, baby. You down? I'm down. Let's go hear some groovy music. Come on. Let's go smoke some dope and hang out with Negroes." He was a pre-Ebonic, medically enhanced wigger!

For now, when it comes to color, all bets are off. You can be anything. When I was a freshman at the University of Michigan, I had a roommate who found out that he was one-eighth Native American. Man, did we party! In the mid-1970s, being Native American, even one-eighth Native American, was like hitting the ethnic lotto. The next morning, he marched right into the financial aid office, and, *wham*, full ride!

The night Barack Obama became president of the United States, something else happened. Not only are black people in, but smart people are in. Power to the nerds! And if you're black *and* smart? Home run. You're a blerd. Election night, Christine grabbed Luisa and started dancing around in front of the TV, holding Luisa's hands up higher and higher, shouting, "Woo hoo! You're in! You're a blerd!"

Wait. My kid is half Korean. She's a Blasian. Damn. I know you're not yet two, but name your college, baby!

It's still hard to get my head around this, though, the idea of acceptance that comes with the Barack Obama presidency. There is a part of me that acknowledges—and remembers, historically—that people of color who tried to deny any part of themselves were suspect. They would have to make a decision and stick with it. If it was found out that they were denying a part of themselves, they would be accused of running away from themselves and be rejected by their own. We're looking at a whole new playing field as of right now. You can embrace all the parts of you. You can say, forthrightly, "I am who I am. I am all my parts," or even, "I am all my parts, but I am embracing this particular one. This is who I am." And we, as a people, will embrace it as well.

I do wonder, though.

What if you are a thirty-year-old brown-skinned African-American man, college-educated, holding a corporate job, married, kids, and you, in this Age of Obama, decide to reveal to your family, friends, and coworkers that you actually identify yourself now as a fourteen-year-old white girl?

"This is who I really am. From now on, please call me Julie. If you need me, text me, or hit me on Facebook. I'll be in my room listening to the Jonas Brothers."

I guess as we go along, we have to draw a line. Create boundaries. I'm not sure if my example of announcing that you are now a fourteen-year-old white girl is an apt one. I suppose there are people who now want to push the envelope. After all, Michael Jackson did that years ago!

For me, I'm comfortable being just black. And while black is in, don't take this wrong, but I am going to take full advantage of it. I am going to spend my political, cultural, and ethnic capital. Why not? The axis of power might be shifting here and I'm going along for the ride. So watch out, white people. In fact, my message to you, while you are still in power, is do not do away with affirmative action or racial quotas, because you're gonna need 'em sooner than you think. When the cultural and ethnic makeup of America changes for good—and we are heading that way fast; according to *Atlantic* magazine, by the year 2042 white people will be the minority—you may just need a little boost. A helping hand. Extra consideration. Some action that is affirmative.

In the meantime, I find there are advantages to being black. Especially when I'm recognized. At the moment, those two together—the combination of being black and having some juice—puts me to the front of the line. People see me, I shoot from last to first.

Well, okay, not everywhere. Not in every line.

Not in restaurants, clubs, the bank, post office, DMV, Starbucks, the bakery, deli, dentist, dry cleaner's, or car wash.

But at airports, watch out!

All the people up front, the baggage handlers at the curb and security guards keeping an eye inside, look out for me. I admit it. I do kind of take advantage of it.

According to the airlines, if you're checking bags, you're supposed to arrive at the terminal an hour and a half to two hours before your plane's scheduled departure.

Not me.

I pull up in my car fifteen minutes before takeoff, sunglasses on, Wu-Tang Clan cranking. I hop out, leave the car running, and head up to the first baggage handler I see, who invariably recognizes me.

"Hey, what's up, DAG?"

"Hey, what's up, man? I have to check my bag. I'm running a little late."

"Don't worry, brother. I got you. Pop your trunk."

"My time is actually pretty tight. My plane leaves in ten minutes."

"No problem. I'm gonna talk to my friend Shirley. She's right up there. See her? Homeland Security? Come on up to the front of the line. Hey, Shirley, hook my man up!"

Shirley waves, walks over, leaving a line of people standing behind a red velvet rope as if she's a bouncer at a club. She smiles at me.

"Ooh, hey, baby. How you doing?"

"What's up, Shirley?"

"I like your little thing that you do."

"Oh, thank you. Thank you very much."

"Well, give me a hug, boo boo."

I give Shirley a hug. She hangs on for what seems like a very long time. With my arms around her, I glance at my watch. Seven minutes until takeoff.

I break Shirley's clench, tap my watch. "Sorry. I'm just a little nervous about making my plane."

"Oh, don't worry about all that. Let me call the pilot."

She whips out a cell phone, punches in a number.

"Hey! Look here, Ronnie. My little friend from TV's coming on. Hold the plane. Okay?" She flips her phone closed. "You all set, boo."

"That's great. Thank you. But what about my car?"

"Oh, I'll park the car. How long you be?"

"Going to New York. Be back in five days."

"Five days? That ain't nothin'. I'll hold the keys for you. Five days, six days, a week. Nothin' to it. When you get off, come see me. I'll have your keys. You know how we do. Give me some sugar."

We hug again. I crack open an eye and squint at my watch. Three minutes to takeoff.

It's not even close. I arrive in plenty of time. Not only does Ronnie the pilot hold the plane but he also hands me a drink as I get on.

Yeah, in the age of Barack, it helps being black, brown, and, especially, beige.

✷   ✷   ✷   **3**   ✷   ✷   ✷

ROYALTY AND HOLINESS

I hear a familiar soft murmur next to me. I glance at Christine. She now has dozed off. Her mouth opens slightly, her warm breath brushes my face. I crane my neck and look out the window into the clouds. Yes. This is real. Unbelievable. But real.

Here I am, flying to Washington, D.C., to attend the inauguration of Barack Obama, the forty-fourth president of the United States. And we're not even paying for it. My wife and I are honored guests. Not only are we going to witness the swearing in of our first black president, be elevated and entertained by the Queen of Soul—

the one and only Aretha Franklin—be touched by the exquisite poetry of Elizabeth Alexander, and be moved, dazzled, and exhilarated once again by the words of Barack Obama, the most inspiring public speaker since Martin Luther King Jr., but we get to do all this for *free.*

We have been given, you see, special tickets. Special *free* tickets. My parents always told me, "David, there is no such thing as a free ride." Well, Mom, Dad, I love you both, and I mean no disrespect, but this one time, you're both wrong. Oh, I had to pay through the nose for our plane tickets and practically donate a kidney for the hotel, but it is well worth it, because we are seeing Barack Obama place his hand on the Lincoln Bible, recite the oath of office, and become president of the United States, in the presence of Michelle, Aretha, and all the other royalty, did I mention, for *free.* I guess, on occasion, being on television does come with perks.

It is strange, but I do feel as if Barack and Michelle exude an air of royalty. I have not felt this way in nearly forty-five years. I settle back in my aisle seat, close my eyes, and remember two moments from my life—my one and only other brush with royalty, and my one brief encounter with holiness.

*   *   *

October 5, 1962. I am seven years old. I live in Detroit, in a neighborhood called Boston-Edison. Contrary to the popular portrayal of Detroit as one big slum, the emblem of urban blight, our neighborhood consists of large, two-story houses nestled on sprawling lawns, each one unique, personal, well-crafted. We have a basement and an attic, several bathrooms, a cook's kitchen, and I have my own bedroom. An easy walk from our house sits a park where housekeepers oversee toddlers in sandboxes or push them on swings, while the older kids play football or duck in and out of the woods playing army.

As a child of the late 1950s and 1960s, I am a product of early television, a fanatic watcher of the black-and-white world of *Sky King, My Friend Flicka, Leave It to Beaver, Father Knows Best,* and, my favorite, for some reason, *The Donna Reed Show.* Although there is scarcely a black face in view, I relate to these families and the houses they live in, the world they inhabit. Outwardly, they reflect my family—Dad, the suit-wearing, briefcase-toting professional; Mom, in charge, petite, dynamic, beautifully coiffed, well-organized homemaker; Geoffrey, my cool, know-it-all older brother; Elizabeth, my pretty, snotty older sister; and me, the youngest, the constant wiseass and sometimes punching bag, the black Beav.

In my family, my parents pushed education ahead of all else. My dad graduated medical school, became a psychiatrist, and ultimately a bestselling author. He—this neighborhood and this house—was living proof of what a good education could bring. Education was, in its own way, our religion. My parents researched the local schools and enrolled us at the Roeper School, the most respected and exclusive private school in the area, located in Bloomfield Hills, a thirty-minute bus ride away.

And so, every morning, beginning in kindergarten, I throw on my school uniform, wolf down breakfast, grab my book bag, and hustle into the backseat of the family car, where my brother pounds me and my sister ignores me while my mother drives us to the bus stop.

This one October morning, my mother backs the car out of the driveway and heads south, away from school, going toward downtown Detroit. My brother has snagged shotgun, my sister's camped behind my mom in the backseat, so I have the right rear window all to myself. I press my face against the glass, blowing circles with my breath.

"Where we going?" I say.

My mother doesn't answer. Her eyes steely with determination, she grips the steering wheel tighter, focuses on the road. She yanks a sharp right, and now we are speeding down a two-lane side street parallel to Woodward Avenue, the main drag in Detroit, twenty-seven miles long, end to end, stretching from downtown and the Detroit River into the suburbs of Birmingham and Bloomfield Hills. We zoom through a neighborhood of smaller two-story houses on rectangular lots, stand-alone garages on each side at the end of slightly inclined driveways. A gap of fifteen to twenty feet separates each garage, and through these spaces I can see Woodward Avenue, a block away. Surprisingly, people have lined up on both sides of the main drag in rows, two and three deep. Why they are here is beyond me, a mystery, but I dare not risk asking my mother, whose concentration behind the wheel has now become almost shaman-like.

I hear a roar from the crowd, and as I glimpse the people on Woodward flashing by through the spaces between the garages, I see them moving forward, straining to see something that's coming. They start to wave, and the roar builds, and I see them floating into these small blinks of space, as if I am watching the motion of a primitive cartoon.

Without warning, my mother slams her foot to the floor and the car blasts off down the street. It feels as if we're flying. My brother's mouth drops open and freezes, my sister hangs on to the door handle with both hands, and I cling to the fabric on the back of the passenger seat. My mother races two more blocks, her head whipping back and forth between the road ahead and the periodic empty spaces that reveal the crowd gathered along Woodward.

And then she slams on the brake and stops the car. In the middle of the street. Across from an opening that gives us a clear view of Woodward.

"Let's go," she says. "Get out of the car."

No arguments, no questions, no hesitation. We scramble out of the car as if it's on fire.

"On the roof!" she shouts, a woman possessed. This time I do hesitate. I start to slump, open my mouth to complain, but before I say a word, she jams her fingers up into my armpits and with a power that belies her small frame heaves me onto the top of the car as if I am a bag of sand. She hauls Elizabeth up next, watches as Geoffrey climbs up himself, and then amazingly she stands up on the hood.

"Get ready," she says.

The roar of the crowd our cue, we stretch our heads toward Woodward, waiting for what?—I'm not sure—but then a motorcade comes into view, a five-car parade, black Cadillac convertibles, with men in suits standing.

"Wave!" my mother commands. "Start waving!"

We do. I wave like a crazy person, both palms flying, and then I add a jump for emphasis. One car passes, and then a second. Then the third arrives, fills the space between the two houses. This car seems to be moving in slow motion. Standing in that car, as if bathed in light, as if a spotlight has illuminated him and only him, is none other than John Fitzgerald Kennedy.

Hatless on this cool October morning, his sandy hair flying, trim and fit in a dark gray suit that seems magically unwrinkled, creased even, he waves back, a slow, deliberate, appreciative wave, accompanied by that now-famous boyish grin, the grin that melts every woman's heart and makes every man feel strong and safe.

I continue to wave and I catch his smile, and I feel, as I'm sure every person lining Woodward feels at that very moment, that JFK is smiling directly at me and only me.

Then he is gone. In a blink.

"That's it," my mother says. "We're done."

We slide down off the roof and get back inside the car. My mother turns on the ignition, taps the steering wheel twice, regards Geoffrey, nods, smiles at Elizabeth, then turns and faces me in the backseat.

"You just saw the president of the United States," she says, firmly, decisively, proudly. "Now you can go to school."

*   *   *

Sunday, June 23, 1963.

Big, important, historic, political event number two in young DAG's life.

Except that I am eight years old and do not give a shit about politics. Or history. Or events. I care about two things. Playing football and eating ice cream. And if I remember to bring some money, I may get lucky and play football at the park and catch the ice cream truck, the same afternoon. Two for one.

It's all about the weekend. Because during the week, my parents make me do my homework after school and limit the times I can meet my friends to play football. But on Saturdays and Sundays, all bets are off.

I wake up this Sunday in June, excited. It's a warm day, which means a perfect day for football and ice cream. Maybe two ice creams. I start to get ready for football, slip on my torn jean shorts and a sleeveless football jersey, when my father comes into my room. My father is six feet four, large, fleshy, and intimidating. He wears a somber look.

"Put on your Sunday clothes," he says. His voice is low and commanding, and his word is law. When my father tells you to do something, there is no wiggle room.

"Why? I'm going to play football—"

"Not today."

Dad never yells. He merely insists. Which, believe me, is more effective than yelling. By anyone.

"We're going to join the march downtown with the Reverend Martin Luther King Jr. Everybody is going."

I know none of my friends are going. They will all be at the park, playing football and eating ice cream. Without me. I sag onto my bed. Lower my head. I feel as if my chin is scraping the floor.

"Why can't I stay home?" I say in a voice just above a whisper.

My father steps into the room. Dad walks with a slight limp, the result of his contracting polio on a troop train when he fought in Korea. The doctors said he would never walk again. He didn't listen to them. At first, he walked with a brace and crutches, then just crutches, then a smaller brace and a cane, and now just the cane, and only on occasion. He will march proudly today, limping and, even if his leg hurts like hell, never complaining. He takes another step into my room. To me it seems as if he blots out the light.

"Look, David, there are going to be a hundred thousand people marching with Dr. King today, for the cause of freedom. One day you'll tell your children that you were there. You'll feel proud. It's important to do this. End of discussion. Now get dressed."

I'm tempted to tell him that I missed the *discussion* part of the discussion, but I elect to hold my tongue. Wise move.

It's a done deal. The whole family gathers with several of our friends, and together we all march with Martin Luther King Jr.

Well, we don't actually walk *with* him.

We don't even see him.

In what is a rare occurrence, a virtually nonexistent event, my father is wrong. There aren't 100,000 people at the march. There are at least 200,000, with some estimates swelling the number closer to 300,000. People are singing, chanting, laughing. At first. Then the heat kicks in and I'm sweating, coughing, complaining.

"I want to go home," I say. "My feet are killing me. My legs hurt. I'm tired."

"Tell Dad," Geoffrey says. "He'll understand."

Suddenly, my mother speed-walks alongside me, her elbows jutting back like wings. There is not a drop of sweat on her.

"Isn't this wonderful?" She is glowing.

"The best," Geoffrey says.

"Oh, David, it's so exciting."

"No, it's not. It's boring. People are pushing me, kicking me. I'm hot. I want to go home."

She considers me, nods with what I want to believe is sympathy.

"David, do you know what's going to happen when you get to the end of the march?"

"Yeah. I'm going to have a heart attack and die."

"No. If you stop complaining, you are going to have ice cream."

I hear a heavenly choir. Celestial voices soar in harmony. A holy light bathes me from above.

"Did you say . . . *ice cream*?"

"I did."

Wow. Another rarity. Because of the heat or the enormity of the day, my mother has gone soft. I got her where I want her. Might as well go for broke.

"Can I have two?"

She doesn't even blink. "I think that can be arranged."

So, on that historic Sunday, June 23, 1963, the day that Martin Luther King Jr. marched side by side with Walter Reuther, president of the United Auto Workers, in one of his famed "freedom marches" before standing in front of over 200,000 people to deliver, for the first time, his "I Have A Dream" speech, perhaps the most famous oration ever spoken, I sit on a curb, oblivious, and slurp *three* ice cream cones, one after another, two courtesy of my mother, one courtesy of my father, who didn't realize I had already scored two from my mother.

My parents are right. I never forgot that day.

✳ ✳ ✳ **4** ✳ ✳ ✳

THE ENVELOPE, PLEASE

I don't know what it is about cabdrivers. They love to talk to me. No, that's not accurate. They *need* to talk to me. And they don't talk: they spew. They open up to me as if I'm their priest, shrink, or barber. All I have to say is, "Hey, what's up?" and they're off and running. It's okay with me. I get some of my best material from cabdrivers.

I think about this as Christine and I look for a cab to take us from Dulles to our hotel. Obama fever is even hotter here on the ground in D.C. than it was at the airport in L.A. Outside the terminal, a swarm of street vendors hits us up with nonstop chatter and a shitload of even more Obama gear and souvenirs, crap that I won't touch but I see that most of the passengers coming off our plane have already gobbled up. In addition to T-shirts, sweats, and headwear in every style and color, they're hawking clocks, key chains, mugs, pens, postcards, calendars, tote bags, teddy bears, snow globes, mouse pads, and refrigerator magnets. Who in their right mind would pay twenty-five dollars for a Barack Obama snow globe?

So I'm sitting in the backseat of the cab holding my snow globe (Christine says Luisa will love it) along with our matching twenty-five-dollar skullcaps and I'm doing the math, calculating that I'm already out seventy-five dollars and we haven't even left the airport, when the cabdriver tilts his head toward the backseat.

"Hey, what's up, DAG? Where you headed?"

"Hey, what's up, man?"

I give him the address of the hotel. He pulls the cab away from the curb. And then he starts. He starts talking nonstop like I'm his shrink and I got a meter running on him instead of the other way around. He talks about the sorry state of D.C., the nation, and the world, then his voice cracks with emotion as he describes how moved and excited he is that Barack Obama is our president. He actually starts to tear up. Then with the stupid snow globe of the White House bouncing in my lap, I start to tear up, which makes Christine roll her eyes.

For some reason, at this moment, I remember another cab ride I took in New York early in the campaign, right after Oprah Winfrey endorsed Obama, the first time she'd ever publicly endorsed a political candidate. Caused something of a stir.

"What do you think of Barack Obama?" I asked that New York cabdriver, an older black man, as we drove through Central Park.

"Ha, ha!" he said. "He is a pimp."

"A pimp?"

"That's right. How'd this brother pull this off? He is a *pimp*. Barack Obama. Lord have mercy. You got to love that."

"Are you gonna vote for him?"

"Of course. I got to. I got to vote for Barack Obama. I got to see what happens. Everyone wanna see what happens with Oprah's pimp."

I ridiculously overtip the cabdriver. Christine looks at me as if I have lost my mind. I give her my helpless—hey, I'm an idiot, what ya gonna do with me—shrug. I try to relate with that shrug what I'm feeling, a very Barack Obama all-inclusive vibe. Hey, we're all in this together. Cabdrivers, comedians, museum curators, politicians. We are all sharing in this beautiful, life-changing, life-affirming moment. This is our day. This is our time.

I feel buoyant as Christine and I walk into the hotel lobby. I have to pause and allow this emotion to sink in.

"It's suddenly hitting me," I say. "We have tickets to Barack Obama's inauguration. Can you believe that?"

"It's incredible. Come on, let's get our room."

"Not yet. I want to bask in the moment. Mannn." I inhale deeply. "We have tickets to the presidential *inauguration*. It's kind of surreal, don't you think? Mind-boggling. Otherworldly. I mean, not everybody gets to go to Barack Obama's inauguration. Well, okay, that's not true. Anybody can go. But not the way we're going. Not invited. Not comped."

"I feel honored. Can we check in?"

"Now, for example, I'm sure, say, Denzel Washington is getting the VIP treatment beyond the VIP treatment we're getting. The ultra-top-level VIP extra. That's totally understandable. Goes without saying. Because he's *Denzel.*"

I scrunch my forehead. Pull off my cap. Scratch my scalp. Weirdest thing. My scalp starts itching when something's bothering me.

Christine sighs. "What's the matter, DAG?"

"I heard that Jamie Foxx is performing for Barack. Tonight, I think. I also heard that he, Spike Lee, and Sam Jackson were invited to breakfast with Barack. Eating breakfast with the president. Is that correct? Don't you think I should've been invited, too?"

Before she can answer, I move past her and stride up to the front desk like I'm the majority owner of the place.

"How are you doing? You're holding a reservation for David Alan Grier."

A young woman dressed all in black with a name tag reading Jillian types something on her flat-screen monitor and smiles.

"There you are. Room 1109. Here are your keys and some general information about the hotel and D.C. Restaurants, directions to the mall, that sort of thing."

She hands me an envelope.

"There actually should be another envelope," I say. "A second envelope. I was told to pick it up when I check in."

Jillian rummages around her station, pulls open a drawer and goes through its contents, bends over, and moves things back and forth on a shelf below her computer screen.

She straightens up, smiles nervously. "Sorry. I don't see anything else. Just the one envelope that we put together from the hotel."

I rake at my head through my cap. "There has to be another envelope, Jillian. There has to be."

Jillian blinks. She sees that I'm about to explode. A look of sheer helplessness mixed with a dash of paralyzing fear clouds her face.

"There is only one envelope, Mr. Grier," she says, and as I open my mouth to speak, she adds, "I swear."

"You don't understand, Jillian. May I call you Jillian?"

Christine lays her hand on my arm.

I lean over the front desk so that I am almost on Jillian's side. I search her station, my eyes scanning the shelf, and every other flat surface in view.

"There . . . is . . . another . . . envelope. Somewhere. It's here . . . someplace. There has to be."

Jillian swallows, loudly. It sounds as if she is drowning. "And what would be in that second envelope?"

"Tickets," I say. "Special tickets. For the inauguration. Special." And then I draw myself up straight as a soldier and say quietly, "We are going to the inauguration. We are invited guests. Jillian, I really need those tickets."

Jillian looks as if she is about to cry. "I am so sorry, Mr. Grier, but I do not have another envelope. That is the only envelope I have." Then she adds, with a hitch of her shoulders, "If it will make you feel better, you can come back here and look for yourself—"

I vault over the front desk.

Jillian backs away, presses herself against the back wall as I frantically rummage through the papers near her computer. Jillian pulls open her drawer and together we empty it out. No envelope. No tickets. I nod, and a whimper escapes from my throat.

"I'm sorry," Jillian says in a quiet, barely audible whimper.

"That's all right," I say in a voice just as small.

I point to my wife, who is standing on the other side of the front desk, looking both stricken and appalled. I turn toward Jillian. I suddenly feel like an eighty-year-old man. I wave at the front desk, which suddenly seems fifteen feet high.

"Getting back. I won't be able to, you know—"

Jillian nods, understanding, and flings opens a restaurant-style swinging door, holding it as I pass through.

A broken man, I walk slowly toward Christine.

"They don't have my tickets," I say.

"I got that," Christine says.

"I bet they were stolen," I say. "That's what happened. The messenger who was supposed to deliver our tickets got mugged on the way over here and somebody ripped off our special tickets and is going to be sitting in our special seats."

I turn back toward Jillian. She cuts me off. "I've been here all day, Mr. Grier. If a messenger got mugged, the company would have called it in."

"David," Christine says. "Call Janet."

Janet. The procurer of the tickets. Of course. She will have the solution to this problem. Probably something simple. Obvious. That's always the case. Bless my wife. Always the voice of reason. Her words spring me into action. I speed-dial Janet's number. She answers on the third ring.

"Hey."

"Janet!" I scream into the phone. "Thank God, listen, I—"

"I'm not available to take your call," Janet's voice continues. "In fact, I'll be unavailable until after the inauguration of *President Barack Obama*. I will be partying hard! Yessss! Oh, and, DAG, enjoy the inauguration and all the festivities, man. I had to sell my sister to get those tickets. Even trade. Later."

Beeep.

I collapse onto a couch in the lobby.

✳   ✳   ✳

I have to go to the inauguration. I have to retrieve my tickets. Somehow. Some way. I have to. For two reasons.

First, my grandmother and my aunt Ethel.

My grandmother used to say, "Dave, if something comes too easy, or sounds too good, that's because it probably is."

She wasn't talking about my tickets to the inauguration, but she could have been.

I loved my grandmother. When I was a little kid, I couldn't wait to see her so that I could snuggle up in her lap and listen to her stories. Seemed like she had a million of them. Mostly she told stories from when she was a child growing up in the segregated South. As I listened, it seemed as if she was describing a long-ago time in a wild kind of country in a faraway land. It was almost as if she was a black Laura Ingalls Wilder. I would sit with her and listen, mouth open, mesmerized, caught up in her tales and her characters, most of whom were my relatives. I found her stories romantic and thrilling. It was only when I got older and more analytical that I saw her stories for what they really were: sad histories, cautionary tales, and, often, horror stories.

My grandmother was the first one to reveal to me that our family, like virtually every other African-American family, including now, most famously, Barack Obama's, was of mixed race. She was in the middle of a story when this fact slipped out. She happened to mention that my great-grandmother was half white. This stopped me cold.

"Half white?" I said. "How did that happen?"

My grandmother paused. Searched for the appropriate words.

"Well, you know, honey, half white. Meaning that your great-great-grandmother was impregnated by a white man."

"What do you mean? Did they date?"

"Uh, no, David, they did not date."

"So they weren't like boyfriend and girlfriend?"

"No, Dave. She was—" My grandmother struggled to find the correct word, a different word. Gave up. "—made pregnant by a white man. Do you understand?"

I stared at her. I just could not comprehend the concept of rape.

"She was powerless," my grandmother said, as if hearing my silent question. "Back then women of color had no choice."

I blurted out, "But couldn't she have told him, 'I don't like you, get away'?"

"It wasn't like that," my grandmother said stiffly, sadly, and repeated, "a woman of color had no choice."

"What happened to her?"

My grandmother sniffed. "A rich white family heard about the baby and sent for him. The mother looked at the child and said,

'That's my son's child.' After a moment, the mother said, 'I will take this child and I will raise this child.'"

My grandmother paused and gently shook a finger.

"Your great-great-grandmother said, 'Absolutely not. I will raise my own child.'"

My grandmother sighed and tears welled up. "She left town with the baby. She met a man. A black man. They fell in love and they decided to get married. The man did not want her to keep the child. See, that would have reflected poorly on him. That would have been his legacy—your wife being raped by a white man. Your great-great-grandmother said, 'If you want me in your life, you have to take us both. Me. And my child.' So he did. They stayed together, had a family, and other children."

"She was very brave," I said.

My grandmother nodded. "Yes, she was. Back then, she had to be."

When I am still in elementary school, my grandmother tells me a story about her sister, my beloved aunt Ethel. Aunt Ethel was my favorite aunt because she always gave me the best presents. In my opinion, the better the present, the better the person. Let's face it. How else do kids rank their favorite relatives?

The story my grandmother tells me about Aunt Ethel thrills me when I hear it because it is so strange. As I grow older, think more about it and process it, the story angers me beyond reason because it is so ugly.

It is a boiling hot summer day. The kind of day in the South where the heat sticks to you like a second skin. Auth Ethel is young, still in her teens. The family lives in Birmingham, Alabama, at the time the heart of the Deep South. One day, Aunt Ethel decides to take the bus to visit some friends and, fittingly, dresses up in her best Sunday clothes.

She gets on the bus and finds a seat, which happens to be in the back of the bus and the only seat left. The bus is packed that day, teeming with passengers. The air is thick, sticky, even hotter than outside, and a sour odor permeates the inside of the bus. The bus leaves the main bus station, drives a few miles, and pulls into its next stop, a run-down, rickety bus station on the outskirts of some backwater. A few people get off, several more get on, including this one white guy. He surveys the passengers who are seated, lumbers through the entire bus, and walks to the back, right over to my aunt Ethel, this nervous teenager. He hitches up his pants and looks down at her.

"You're sitting in my seat," he says. "Get up and give it to me. And since that seat is the last one on the bus, you're gonna have to get off."

Aunt Ethel looks out the window, sees nothing but barren and parched ground for miles.

"I can't get off here," she says, standing, her voice shaking. "We're in the middle of nowhere."

The white man shrugs. "That's too bad."

He pushes past her and sits heavily down on what was her seat. The bus lurches forward, then grinds to a stop. In his rearview mirror, the bus driver has caught a glimpse of Aunt Ethel standing in the middle of the aisle. He mumbles something under his breath, jerks up the emergency brake, and walks back to Aunt Ethel.

"You have to get off the bus," he says to Aunt Ethel. "You ain't allowed to stand. They's the rules."

"You can't leave me stranded," Aunt Ethel pleads. "There's nothing out there. Not even a town. Please."

"Either you get off the bus," the bus driver says, "or ride under the bus."

"What . . . what do you mean . . . under?"

"In the luggage bin."

"You're gonna make me ride with the suitcases?"

"Won't charge you extra neither."

When I think of that story now, I know it's a horrible story. Dehumanizing, humiliating, enraging.

And yet, the way my grandmother told it and the way I heard it—at least when I was a little kid—the story sounded crazy. Even . . . funny. I saw Aunt Ethel as a strange kind of heroine, and I pictured the world she lived in as the Wild, Wild West.

Aunt Ethel turns and glares at the white man who's taken her seat, storms past the bus driver, climbs down off the bus, and, with as much dignity as she can muster under these circumstances, yanks down the luggage compartment and lies down on top of a bed of suitcases. The bus driver arrives, sees her lying there, starts to say something. Aunt Ethel holds her arms daintily across her chest and turns her head. The bus driver closes the luggage compartment flap, climbs back behind the wheel, and drives off.

But the worst part?

He forgets about her.

Aunt Ethel stays locked in the luggage compartment of that bus for two hours. It seems impossible, but nobody hears her banging, kicking, and screaming. Finally, a couple of men from the bus company open the luggage compartment door and find Aunt Ethel lying there, her dress torn, sweat-soaked, and stained beyond repair, her makeup a runny mess, her breathing coming fast and hard.

"Bus driver forgot you was in there," one of the men says.

"We thought we heard something," the other man admits. "We wasn't sure."

"Thought it was the road," the first man says. "You know gravel or some loose sticks banging up against the bus's belly—"

Aunt Ethel rolls out of the luggage compartment. She struggles to stand, staggers, reaches out, and leans on the bus to stop from falling. The two men just stand there and watch. Neither one helps her. Aunt Ethel, tears streaming down her face, pushes past the two bus company guys, trying to find a semblance of dignity.

So, see, I have to find my purple tickets and go to Barack Obama's inauguration, for my grandmother and for Aunt Ethel.

They are reason number one.

*   *   *

Reason number two lies asleep on my lap. Curled up into my chest.

Luisa Danby Grier Kim.

A year old. In Korean, *Danby* means "gentle rain." It may be a coincidence, but to me there is nothing more soothing than a gentle rain falling, and there is nothing more calming and beautiful than watching my daughter lying here with me, her breath brushing my forearm. I'm at peace.

We sit in front of the TV, watching John King on CNN. He stands beside his beloved pale blue delegate map of the United States. In a moment, John King will do what he loves best. He will press his palm onto his precious touch-screen delegate map and update the states, make them change color. He lives for this. And, strangely, so do I.

But John King of CNN cannot just touch the map without a buildup, without explanation, without creating anticipation and expectation. It would be like telling a joke with only the punch line.

Wait. Here it comes! John King raises his hand, edges it closer to the screen. He looks as if he's about to press the map. Nope. It's just a tease. He's circling the Midwest, dangling his fingers tantalizingly above Minnesota and Wisconsin. His hand is hovering. He turns now to the camera and talks about Barack Obama and how, to everyone's amazement, especially Hillary Clinton's, he has captured a surprising amount of widespread, mainstream support, especially in states with caucuses. And, unlike previous African-American presidential candidates like Jesse Jackson and Al Sharpton, who stirred things up and then faded away, Barack Obama is actually coming on.

Now, postscript. Full disclosure. I have to admit that when Barack Obama announced his candidacy, I—like most black folks and people of color I knew—didn't think he had a chance.

I said to myself, *He's too young. Too new. Too liberal. It's not his time. It's gonna be Hillary Clinton. He might even be wasting his chance.*

I thought all of this. I'm still skeptical.

But then John King on CNN waves his hand over entire chunks of the United States. "Again, the total number of delegates needed to win the nomination is two thousand one hundred and seventeen, and tonight as we look at our interactive, fluid, ever-changing touch screen—"

He's going in! He's pressing states! Turning them dark Obama blue!

"As you see," John King says, his fortress of silver hair flapping slightly as he touches the map of America, "after Super Tuesday, there has been a shift. Let's look at Connecticut, Maine, Illinois, Kansas, Minnesota, Missouri, Wisconsin, Nebraska, Utah, Georgia, Louisiana, Virginia, Maryland, North Carolina, Utah, and the state of Washington. If we count all those for Obama, and those are very possible, more than possible, likely, and if we move—"

Luisa stirs. Nuzzles against my cheek. Opens her mouth, sighs, squawks.

Time whips ahead. Thirty seconds. A minute. I can't be sure. I just know that John King has thrown the discussion over to a panel of hosts and pundits, many of them with two last names—Anderson Cooper, Campbell Brown, Wolf Blitzer—who are nodding and pontificating and predicting, and as Luisa wriggles around to get comfortable I hear overlapping voices in the background say, "Highly organized campaign," and "Brilliant strategy in the caucuses," and "It all started with Iowa," and then somebody says—Gergen, I think, or maybe Toobin—"You know, I'm gonna go out on a limb here, but— if everything falls in place, just like on your map, John—Barack Obama could actually win this nomination."

I start to cry.

Sitting in front of John King's interactive touch-screen map of the United States, the darker shades of blue representing states committed to Obama, I begin to sob. And then I say aloud to the CNN political team, "Oh, my God, this could happen."

The political team is talking over each other, pointing at the map, fighting to express their punditry, and someone manages to shout above the rest, "Well, wait, if he loses this state, and that state falls the way we predict it will . . . no, no, you're right, even if that happens, he can still, yes, even then, he still has enough delegates for the nomination, no matter how you do the math—"

I cry harder.

I look down at Luisa, who lies still, her eyes wide open, staring up into mine, searching, it seems.

And I know that this is the moment when everything has changed.

The whole world has changed.

We, as a nation, as a culture, are going in a different direction.

The revolution has begun.

The symbol of the revolution is not what I expect.

The symbol of the revolution shocks me.

The symbol is not an angry speech from an angry black leader like H. Rap Brown. The emblem is not a Black Power fist thrust into the air by Stokely Carmichael. The symbol is not a protest or rally led by Malcolm X.

The symbol of the revolution is John King's interactive touch-screen map that changes when his flying fingers turn a cluster of midwestern states dark blue.

Through my tears, I look down and lock eyes with my daughter. She is looking up at me with wonder. I think, *Wow. I can't wait to tell her. I can't wait to share this with her.*

Because from this moment on, I know that her world will be different from mine.

I close my eyes and rock her against my chest.

★ ★ ★ 5 ★ ★ ★

PUBLIC THERAPY

Election Day. November 4, 2008.

Restless night. Luisa fussy. I get up and pace with her back and forth through the house, rock her gently, sing to her softly. She's calm when I hold her and sing. But as soon as I put her down, she starts to wail. I get it. She's nervous about the election. I don't blame her. I am, too.

We've never come this close. All the pundits on TV and online say that the numbers, the math, add up to an Obama victory, maybe even a landslide. Still, I can't help worrying about the Bradley Effect.

In 1982, Tom Bradley, former Los Angeles mayor, an African-American, ran for governor. According to the polls leading up to the election, Bradley had the election locked up. Californians went to bed thinking that they would wake up to the state's first black governor. Didn't happen. Bradley lost. Apparently, for the first time ever, white people lied. When pollsters at polling places asked them who they'd voted for, they said, "Who do you think? The black guy. Bradley. He's my man," when in fact they'd gone the other way.

So, yeah, I'm worried about the Bradley Effect.

I'm also worried about what I'm going to say in front of one thousand people if Obama loses.

I've been asked to host the Democratic election night party being held in the main ballroom at the new Hyatt Regency in Century City. I've been preparing jokes for days. Here's what I've got, based on a rant I did on the *Chocolate News*:

> *Black people, check the time, check the date, and check yo-self. We are within spittin' distance of putting one of our own in the White House. I know you wanna express your joy that we've made it this far, but trust me, making the national anthem more black and calling for a race war if Barack loses tonight will not help. And if Barack wins, we gotta do everything we can to keep white people comfortable with a black president. Certain black celebrities really need to watch their step. For instance—*

FLAVA FLAV . . . Your ass needs to go on hiatus.

TERRELL OWENS . . . You need to hand the football back to the ref after you score and stop yelling at your coach on the sidelines.

NAOMI CAMPBELL . . . Stop slapping the shit outta people. Matter of fact, put your bitch slapping hand on hiatus. Lock yourself in a cellar.

SERENA WILLIAMS . . . Start losing.

KANYE WEST . . . Quit smashing people's cameras.

JEREMIAH WRIGHT . . . Go somewhere and hide.

OPRAH . . . Don't change a thing. Baby, keep doin' yo lil' book club.

Now, I'm not just talking about celebrities. Everyday brothers and sisters, we gotta keep white people smiling, too. So laugh at Larry the Cable Guy. Pretend you get Neil Diamond. And tell anyone who will listen that, yes, Eminem is the greatest rapper of all time. And above all else, if you get into a car accident with a white person and it's not even close to your fault, don't shout, scream, or even honk the horn. Get out, laugh at the dents in your brand-new Chrysler 300, and say, "Chet, it happens to all of us . . . Hope and Change!"

Get it? PLAY THE GAME!

In exchange, after a few months, I promise you, we can let loose and you can pretend that America is your own Source Awards after-party. Feel free to go crazy, light shit on fire, and return Bobby Brown's phone calls. After all, what are they gonna do . . . call the president? Ha-ha! Too late, motherfuckers!

Feels funny. Then I realize . . . what if he loses? I may be too depressed to be funny.

That's not true.

I *will* be too depressed to be funny.

I do have a plan. If he loses, I'm not showing up. People will understand. Hell, they ain't gonna show up either. Nobody's gonna wanna party. We'll all be home doing the same thing after we get over our hysterical crying and someone hoses us down: we'll be renting a U-Haul, packing up everything we own, and moving the hell outta here. I can deal with Canada. I won't even say I'm black. Standing next to Christine, I'll be hoping to pass for Korean.

The day drags on. I get up, kill time, answer e-mails, go to the gym, vote, and head over to the studio, where I, optimistically, work out some more stuff that I'll say at the party. All this time CNN drones on, popping back and forth between pundits, periodically throwing over to John King on the sidelines, poised like a *Jeopardy!* contestant over his touch-screen map. Around six o'clock, the first results come in, and, wouldn't you know it, CNN announces that John McCain has taken West Virginia.

"Here we go," I mutter, as John King's palm turns West Virginia red. Blood red.

"Why don't you keep your damn hands in your got-damn pockets, John King!" I yell at the screen, as if his hands pressing his precious touch-screen map is the reason John McCain has won West Virginia.

Then, stunningly, one by one, the states fall to Obama—Massachusetts, Connecticut, Maine, New Hampshire, New York—and I know. I just know. It's over. Done deal. He's gonna win.

"I was never worried," I say.

Then everything starts to amp up. I go from calmly watching CNN and jotting down jokes to feeling the atmosphere around me shift into a frenzy.

"We'd better get you over to the party," someone says.

I check my watch. It's not quite 6:30.

"Kinda early," I say.

"They're telling us it's getting crazy over there. Traffic's horrendous, backed up. People out on the streets. Like *crazy* crazy."

The drive from the studio to Century City usually takes twenty minutes. Tonight, it takes almost an hour. More traffic than usual? Possibly. More people walking the streets? Looks like it. But that's not what makes the drive longer. What I sense is that the emotion of the moment, the impending joy, is causing cars and people to clog up the streets because they are moving slower, not faster. It's as if people don't want to jump the gun, don't want to get too excited too soon. It's not official. No one has made any kind of announcement. John McCain is still holed up in his hotel. He hasn't conceded anything. Barack Obama is in lockdown in Chicago, supposedly hanging out a short walk from Grant Park. He has not claimed victory. Too early. Polls are still open. Even though we all feel what's about to happen.

So we move in slow motion.

Things pick up, hit another gear as we approach Century City. When we pull onto the Avenue of the Stars, we are met by a sea of people lapping up toward the Hyatt Regency. They are in high spirits, people attending a massive pep rally. The air crackles in high anticipation. It's as if we are all trapped inside a giant, invisible champagne bottle, just waiting for someone to pop the cork and let us out.

As we get closer to the hotel, the crowd swells. Creeping forward, our car inches through the mass of humanity. I squint through the window and focus on the faces. Amazing. We've got it all covered here—all different ages, colors, races. They are chanting, "Obama! Obama!" and "Yes, We Can!" I don't hear, see, or feel an iota of anger.

Do not witness a speck of rage. Nothing happening here but sheer, unadulterated joy. Heading toward a whole cloud cover of bliss.

A surge. The crowd rushes toward the main lobby of the Hyatt Regency and is halted by a line of police. Now here comes some even weirder shit. The cops aren't angry, either! L.A. cops, not angry? I have videotapes of L.A. cops pounding on people. Black people, mostly. L.A. cops are born angry. And mean. And unnaturally attached to their nightsticks. Not these cops. Not tonight. They're cool, calm, wearing expressions that read "Hey, people, we're just doing our jobs. We got these damn pesky fire laws to enforce. Otherwise, you know we'd let you in to rampage the place. But, hey, we're with you. Chillin'."

Crazily enough, this crowd tonight seems content to stay out here and chill and, eventually, in the not-too-distant future, celebrate.

Inside the car, cell phones beep, vibrate, a flurry of calls and texts coming in. The driver pulls the car over to the curb and tilts his head back toward me.

"There are so many people the police had to shut the party down fifteen minutes ago," he says. "Can't let anyone else in and can't get close to the lobby. So we're gonna take you in from here."

He squeezes out of the car, shimmies through the crowd, and somehow manages to pry open my door. Like a couple of running backs, we duck, dip, and weave our way through the mass of bodies, find the side entrance of the hotel.

"How many people are out here?" I ask. "Anybody get a number?"

"They say between five and ten thousand and growing," the driver says.

"Damn," I say.

Inside, it feels like *more.*

The ballroom is packed end to end with people—again, all sizes, ages, colors, races. Wall-to-wall exuberance with just the slightest hint of hesitation—as if everyone's still waiting for the lid to come off—shakes the house. As I come in, Senator Barbara Boxer stands on a stage at the far end of the ballroom, in the middle of a speech, a diminutive figure in a smart victory suit. Behind her a huge screen projects CNN election coverage, Wolf, Anderson, Campbell, Soledad, and all the rest, including, of course, John King and his touchscreen map of America, the states now turned sky blue and apple red, bathing the senator in their massive shimmering shadows. The possibility of Barack Obama's victory—his historic, unprecedented journey and South Side of Chicago rags-to-riches story—has inspired Senator Boxer at this moment to share with us her story. I'm sure it's a fascinating, heartwarming, up-from-the-bootstraps story, one that I'm dying to hear . . . *just not tonight.*

"And then I bought my first pair of heels," the senator muses. "They didn't fit, my feet swelled—"

Behind her, a mammoth Wolf Blitzer, his giant, frightening face filling the entire back wall, suddenly swallows Senator Boxer whole. He opens his mouth and he says—I swear I detect the slightest trembling of his bottom lip—"CNN now projects Barack Obama president of the United States!"

Pandemonium.

Nonstop, ear-shattering screaming.

A freaking freak-out. Bananas.

People losing their minds.

Forget losing their minds. People losing their bodies. Hell, people losing their whole *selves.*

It is like some religious phenomenon. As if the spirit hits this crowd, this wall-to-wall mass of people, every one of them, and takes them over. Inhabits them. Makes them lose control.

People everywhere, sobbing, wailing, writhing.

Out. Of. Their. Heads.

I stand in the center of it all. Staring at the giant CNN screen. I want to make sure. I want to be absolutely certain this isn't a mistake. Some kind of cruel Republican practical joke—

Wolf (hand to his ear): "Wait a minute, wait a minute. I've just been handed a note. It's all a mistake. John McCain is the president of the United States!"

Rush Limbaugh (his chubby head crashes through the middle of John King's touch-screen map): "HAHA*HA*, WOLF!! YOU HAVE JUST BEEN PRANKED!!"

But, no. It's real. This is happening. People I've never seen before throw their arms around me. Women—and men—kiss me. A young staff photographer, black kid I've seen around, drops his camera to the floor and starts leaping up and down, up and down, screaming. A white woman, tears streaming down her face, staggers toward me, raises her arms to the ceiling, and faints. She lies on the floor out cold. People step over her, around her, crying, howling, clapping.

Scattered phrases fly by me, machine-gun fast: "Cannot believe this is happening"; "Never in my lifetime"; and variations of, "Oh my God, I can die now, everything is going to change, hope and change, we did it, he did it, OHMYGOD!!!"

I stand, eyes still riveted on the huge screen, images of Barack Obama waving, hugging Michelle, hugging his campaign team members. My legs feel as if they are clamped to the floor, embedded in cement. I cannot move. I blink, and Barack Obama—President-elect Barack Obama—is waving and grinning right at me, just the way JFK waved at me, and only me, from that motorcade forty-five years ago.

The guy in charge of tonight's event, a thin headset strapped to him as if he's a security guard or a Justin Timberlake backup dancer, approaches, anxiety riding him all over.

"Little change of plan," he toots in what I'm sure is not his normal voice.

"Okay," I say, going along, not sure where this is headed.

"You know, because everything is so fluid."

"Uh-huh."

"We're already in high gear. The thing has launched. We are in go position."

"Right."

I nod, smile.

I have no idea what he's talking about.

"So, Plan B. John McCain's gonna give his concession speech."

"Sure. It's customary."

"Then Barack Obama's gonna speak."

Again, I nod. "The acceptance speech. From Grant Park. Amazing."

Now he's nodding. "Then you go on."

I pause for what feels like an hour.

"What?" I finally say. "Go on and do *what*? This is a tumultuous, insane . . . insanity. I'm not going on. I am not about to follow the first black president. I'll be like those Swedish acrobats who followed The Beatles on *The Ed Sullivan Show*."

"David, please."

Now I get it. This has something to do with his job. It has to. Because now this guy is shaking.

"Please," he says again. "Just go on. They'll love it. Please."

"I don't have anything to say. I mean, I'm just . . . happy. I have only . . . happiness. I got nothing."

"You have to go on. You have a contract. My boss made me say that."

The next hour flies by at warp speed. McCain speaks. A gracious concession. It is the best moment of his presidential run. Then Barack Obama speaks. Stirring, emotional, vintage Barack. He soars. And then—

"Ladies and gentlemen, put your hands together for our host . . . DAVID ALAN GRIER!"

The crowd applauds. I hop onto the stage, wave, and blurt out, "Bush, I hope you got the U-Haul backed up to the White House, because you're gone and we're in!"

Huge applause.

As they're applauding, I remember appearing with Adam Carolla on his radio show and breaking down the clichés everyone says at political rallies: "Lower taxes. More jobs. Health care for everyone."

"Say these things and you'll never go wrong," Adam jokes on the air with me.

So I say them.

Even more applause!

Then I look at the crowd looking up at me and I just decide to be completely honest, to tell them exactly how I feel. I decide to follow my heart. I decide not to *perform*.

"I don't know about you all, but I just got to scream!" I shout. "Not '*Yes, we can*' . . . YES, WE DID!"

The crowd screams with me.

"Not '*Four more years*' . . . EIGHT MORE YEARS!"

The crowd is going insane.

I lower my head, then lower my voice. I lift my head up and try to blink away the tears that are filling my eyes.

"You know, I remember my grandmother telling me stories about the world she grew up in. It was a very different world, and it wasn't all that long ago—"

I can't finish. My voice sticks in my throat. I'm really crying now. I can barely speak.

Somehow, with great passion, I manage to say, "I never thought— I *never* thought—that I would live to see what has happened tonight. Not in my lifetime."

I look out into the crowd and I see a wave of people clustered up at the stage, and *they're* all crying. Crying with me. I hear their voices coming up at me, encouraging me, cheering me on: "Let it go, let it go, it's all right, let it go—"

So I do.

That night—after I've allowed myself this public display of emotion, offered myself up as the focus of a group-therapy-cheer-on, sobbed, wailed, let every emotion inside me flow—I go home, hug my wife, hold her, and say, "What a night, Christine, what a night. It's not stopping tonight. Baby, we're going. We are going to the inauguration. We are going to bear witness. I don't care what it costs, what I have to do. We are *going*."

I got to find those got-damn tickets.

★ ★ ★ **6** ★ ★ ★

DEATH OF THE
ANGRY BLACK MAN

According to certain African-American scholars, prominent spokespersons, and "experts" on the subject, since Barack Obama has been elected president of the United States, I have to stop making fun of black people. It has become my responsibility to uplift the race.

Point taken.

I come on *Chocolate News* and say, "Whatever you do, black people, stop doing stupid shit. In fact, don't do *anything*. And you ghetto-ass people, don't dress like that. Put the pimp cup down."

I'm doing my part.

But then I get an e-mail that says, "Black people, I call on all of us. Please, whatever you do, don't make jokes about Barack Obama and the First Family. They may be very funny, even hilarious—and we all want to laugh—but we can't."

Hey, far be it from me to make fun of the first black president. Not gonna happen.

On the political and practical front, however, I do have to question one of his first policy decisions.

I heard that he has agreed to have his mother-in-law move into the White House with him.

A black mother-in-law living with him? Well, we know one thing for damn sure.

He's not getting away with shit.

I wish I could have been a fly on the wall when Michelle first brought up the subject.

"Barack, we did it! You are president and I am First Lady. I'm so proud of you. I love you so much. Oh, by the way, my mother is moving in with us."

"What?"

"You heard me. My mother's moving in. The kids are so happy. You think you can take off a couple hours tomorrow to help her move?"

"Are you out of your *mind*? Your mother is not gonna live with us."

"Oh, yes she is."

"I become president and this is what I get? I'm putting my foot down. She is not moving in."

"She's not? Fine. Then I'm not either."

"Michelle, do you not know that I am now the leader of the free world?"

"You may be. But you are not the leader of this house."

"But your mother can—"

"My mother can what?"

"Never mind. I am getting so aggravated over this. Fine, whatever. Let her move in. Just keep her away from Cabinet meetings. And briefings on the economy. And press conferences. Especially keep her away from press conferences."

"Excuse me. My mother can *what*?"

He may be able to declare war, but this is one battle he is never gonna win.

✳ ✳ ✳

Now that Barack Obama is president, I'm afraid that it means the death of the angry black man. Too bad. The angry black man was an institution. An archetype. His death signals the end of an era. We are all kinder and gentler now.

Shit.

As a kid, I was attracted to the image of the angry black man. He projected a persona that was fiery, sexy, rebellious, and powerful— exactly what I wanted to be. Angry black men were my idols. I'm talking about angry black men such as . . .

Mohammad Ali.

He was cool, flamboyant, crazy, and an outlaw. He would dance around you in the ring, recite poetry, slap you, and then when he felt like it, knock you the fuck out.

Malcolm X.

There was no scarier African-American in the world. He was calm, eloquent, logical, intelligent—shit, he wore *glasses*—and he still scared the hell out of white people.

Linc Hayes.

That's right. Linc from *The Mod Squad,* played by Clarence Williams III. A seriously angry black man. One of my true idols. And he wasn't even real.

A key moment in my life. Tuesday, September 24, 1968. The phone rings. It's one of my brother's friends.

"Geoffrey, turn on the TV," he says. "There's a brotha on this show called *The Mod Squad* and he ain't taking no shit."

We run to the TV, tune in ABC, and there is Linc. Black sunglasses and huge Afro. We are stunned, in awe.

"Man," I say to Geoffrey, "who would wear hair like that?"

In the show, to cops and criminals alike, all Linc says, eyes behind his shades, is basically, "Fuck you." In the run of the show, five years, he essentially never speaks, except to say, "Yeah? Fuck you."

Oh, I didn't want to be like Linc; I wanted to *be* Linc.

Finally, there was H. Rap Brown, one of the founders of SNCC (Student Nonviolent Coordinating Committee), who later became a higher-up in the Black Panthers. Rap was hard core. He even made it onto the FBI's Ten Most Wanted List. He would say shit like, "Violence is as American as apple pie," and "If America don't come around, we're gonna burn it down."

He was a bad mother . . . shut yo mouth!

When I was about eleven years old, I saw him on TV giving a no-torious news conference from Cambridge, Maryland, which would result in his being arrested for inciting to riot. He stood in front of a group of reporters, who peppered him with questions. One guy asked, "Are you gonna go to the Cambridge city hall?"

Rap said, "Honky, I haven't decided where the fuck I'm going."

I was enraptured. Rap was on the attack, and he was fucking awesome. I sat on the floor, glued to the TV. Another reporter dared to ask him a follow-up question.

"Sir, did you really say that you wanted to shoot the president of the university?"

"Hey, honky, I may shoot you."

I couldn't believe the shit this guy was saying. He was so profane, so confrontational, so dangerous. I couldn't process it at the time, but looking back, you can see where the voice of hip-hop came from—out of the mouth and mind of the angry black man.

*   *   *

The election of Barack Obama may mean the end of the angry black man, but it's not just black people who should be responsible for the death of that image. White people have to do their part as well.

Full disclosure.

I am not an angry black man, even though I play one on TV.

But, white people, you have a long way to go to understand this.

You *see* me as an angry black man. Even now. After all this time, all these years. Even in this supposedly postrace world.

Recently, I was enjoying some much needed R&R one weekend in Laguna Beach, a resort town between L.A. and San Diego. It is around eight at night, starting to get dark, and I'm standing on a corner waiting for the light to change so I can cross. I'm wearing a baseball cap and baggy clothes. The light turns green, I start to walk across the street, and I see this older white couple in their car check me, lock their doors—*clank*—and drive off.

This gets to me.

I run after them.

I start screaming, "It's okay! It's okay! I'm on TV! I'm an actor!"

I can only imagine what they are thinking, catching me in their rearview mirror, sprinting like a fool, trying to catch up to them, waving like a maniac.

"Oh, my God, he's coming after us. Floor it, Stanley."

"Wait!" I scream. "Hold up! Don't be afraid! I'm not like the rest of them! Wait!!!"

Hope and change.

I hope that with Barack as president now we can change this shit.

For a while, I desperately wanted to be an angry black man. This was beyond a career choice. I believed it was my true ambition. My goal in life. My calling.

I was ten.

And I was really angry.

For the most part, anger kept its distance from our house. It was pretty much a foreign emotion. I never saw much of it around.

Well, I did want to kill my brother, and my brother wanted to kill me, but that went way past anger; that went into the realm of brutality, violence, and vengeance. What I felt came under the heading of good, old-fashioned older-brother-younger-brother *I will kick your fucking ass* hatred. My brother kicked my ass on a regular basis just because he was older and he could. He would bide his time, wait for my mother to leave for a club meeting or go out shopping. As soon as she pulled the car out of the garage, he would haul the pillows off the living room couch, toss them on the floor to create a makeshift combo wrestling mat and boxing ring, and commence the pounding of my ass. I would fight back, lose, cry, and silently plot my revenge. I'd wait a day or two, let him think I forgot, lull him into complacency. Then late at night when I was sure he was asleep, I'd tiptoe into his room and smash him over the head with his wire wastebasket. I would then run like hell and lock myself in my room, because I knew that once he snapped out of his coma, he was going to kill me. One time he came to in the middle of my pummeling him and swatted the wastebasket out of my hand. He lunged for me. Missed. I bolted. Flew down the stairs. His arms pumping, his eyes wild, he chased me through the entire house. I cut left, right, zigged and zagged like Reggie Bush. My brother gained on me. I picked up speed, skidded into the kitchen, and raced for the back door, which was closed. I didn't care. I plowed right through it, splintering the wood, shattering the glass.

Except for fight night with my brother, the atmosphere in our house lay thick with the constant hanging layer of quiet dignity. I rarely heard my parents argue, never saw them fight; I can't recall either one of them raising their voices. I vaguely remember one argument that my parents had when I was eight or nine. I heard a distant door close and I remember my mother coming into the living room, and I noticed that she was crying. The next night at dinner my mother called a family meeting. She announced in a quiet, proper way that she and my father were having "problems."

"It has nothing to do with you," she assured us.

My father said nothing. He let my mother carry the ball on this one.

"We're working everything out, nipping it in the bud," my mother added. "We just wanted you to know, as a family, that we're dealing with it, working through it. That's all."

I didn't hear anything more about their "problems" for several more months, until my mother told us that my father was moving out.

He'd decided to relocate to San Francisco. If I had been older, I would have identified what he was experiencing as a midlife crisis. But instead of purchasing a sports car and running off with a twenty-two-year-old, he bought himself a dashiki and decided to become a hippie. A practicing psychiatrist who'd just turned that classically dangerous age of forty, my father was entering a flower-child phase. He was beginning a new life. Only he wasn't taking any of us with him.

He was going to find himself in San Francisco. My mother—ever dignified, polite; the good wife—not only supported my dad's decision but she also helped him pack. In stunned silence, I watched them load all of my father's clothes, books, and other belongings into moving boxes, and then, amazingly, before she sealed the boxes for good, she lovingly sprayed Right Guard over all his clothes so that they would smell fresh when he unloaded the boxes in San Francisco, on the other side of the country.

I couldn't comprehend this separation, couldn't wrap my head around the need for him to leave or the logic behind it. I just knew, though, that it was temporary. Something of the moment. Maybe not even real. I figured that my father would cool off or drop out in San Francisco, to me the coolest city on the planet, recharge his battery, or whatever else needed recharging, and come home.

He never did. He settled in San Francisco, wrote my mom a Dear John letter saying that he was moving on, and that was that.

Divorce.

The word didn't even sound real. It felt foreign, as if it had been part of some strange, other language. Of course, I'd heard the word a million times. In the '60s people in our neighborhood were divorcing right and left. Seemed like dudes were packing up and leaving every day. It just never occurred to me that *divorce* would become a word that I would have to incorporate into my vocabulary, a word that I would have to use to describe part of my life. Divorce happened to other people, to people around me, not to me. Not to my parents. I couldn't really comprehend what it meant. It was like other words that I knew but couldn't comprehend, like *assassination.* Sure, I knew the meaning of the word. I could define it. I just couldn't make the word apply to me, to my life.

My parents' divorce shook me to my core. I felt betrayed, sad, abandoned, and angry. Incredibly sad, and really, really angry.

David, use your new vocabulary words in a sentence.

Okay. Let's see.

When my parents got a divorce, *I might as well have been* assassinated.

My father came back to Detroit for Christmas that year. I had been crying a lot. Seemed like 24/7. I was ten years old, and when I thought of my father and mother's split, I would just lose it. My mother asked my father to talk to me during the Christmas visit. He was a psychiatrist, after all.

On Christmas Eve, he took me for a ride. We drove slowly through the neighborhood, taking in all of the Christmas lights. Neither of us spoke much. I could feel him struggling to find the right thing to say.

"David," he said after a while, "you know how it is when you start school, and you have a new teacher?"

"Sure."

"And you really like that teacher at the beginning of the year? You with me?"

"Yeah."

"But then you find out, say around midway through the year, that you don't really like that teacher anymore. She's not what you thought. Do you know what I mean?"

"Yes."

"Well, that's what happened with your mother and me."

My ten-year-old mind strained to comprehend my father's logic. I couldn't do it. I felt lost.

"But Mom's not a teacher," I said. "She's my mother."

The rest of the conversation is a blurry mix of my father's frustration and my tears. He tried to reason with me, tried to explain himself, and I tried desperately to understand. But even as he comforted me, I could feel the anger welling up. Finally I just blurted, "You're not being a good father. You're not taking care of us."

He drove me home. We had nothing more to say to each other. He would go back to San Francisco with the issue between us unresolved. To my mind, he would never adequately explain why he moved away and left our family. And I, of course, was too young to begin to fathom the vagrancies of the human heart.

I just knew that he was gone and that I was angry.

*   *   *

I am twelve. My dad now calls San Francisco home. We stay connected through phone calls and annual visits. He gives up being a hippie doctor and coauthors a book, *Black Rage,* which climbs up the bestseller lists and lands him on television and radio talk shows. It's strange seeing my father as a real live angry black man and semi-celebrity. I'm proud and a little in awe, but honestly, I don't give it too much thought. Mainly because I'm too busy trying not to get my ass kicked every day in junior high school.

When my father moved out, my mother had to make some difficult financial adjustments, which mainly required our family to learn how to live on a lot less money. The first thing to go, as she explained in a family meeting, was private school. No way could she afford three private school tuitions *and* three college tuitions. The one promise she made to us, and to herself, was that all three of us were going to college. That was nonnegotiable, a deal breaker. She would move into our dorm room with us if she had to. But we were all going to college.

Right now, at twelve, college is the furthest thing from my mind as I ride one of two buses I take back and forth from my new junior high school, a wild-ass, mini version of the HBO show *Oz*. At least it feels that way to me compared to my old private posh suburban elementary school, where, in the event of conflict, we were always encouraged to use our words instead of our fists. I can just see some of the kids here at Oz out there at Roeper in Bloomfield Hills.

"Dwayne! Why did you slap David? We don't slap. And we don't head butt. Use your words. What would you like to say to David?"

"Use my words? Arright. Yo, David. After school. Three o'clock. I'm gonna fuck you up, you candy-ass, piece of shit motherfucker!"

At Wildass Junior High, I train my G.I. system as if I'm a POW. I learn to survive from 7:00 a.m. to 3:00 p.m. without even thinking about taking a shit at school. The last place you want to end up sitting unprotected is on the toilet in junior high school. You have to be on high alert every second—in the hall, on the playground, even in class. And the potential ass kicking doesn't end on school grounds. You have to watch your ass on the bus, too. At Wildass, I have my share of fights. Not because I enjoy fighting; I don't. I enjoy staying alive.

Most of my fights last less than twenty seconds and are exactly the same. No weapons of any kind. No blades (guns were unheard of), sticks, rocks, rolls of quarters, baseball bats, or tools you took from shop class. No sand tossing in the face, nose or eye gouging, biting, or kicking in the balls. That shit is off limits. Not allowed. Unfair and unsportsmanlike. Just punching, kicking, wrestling, and choking. Whatever we can get in twenty seconds.

Every fight starts with a spirited, back and forth, in-depth discussion:

"Fuck you!"

"No, fuck you!"

"No. FUCK YOU!"

"NO. FUUUUUUCCCCKKKKK YOUUUUUU!"

"Tomorrow, motherfucker!"

"Three o'clock!"

"Right here!"

"I'm gonna fuck you up!"

"I'm gonna fuck YOU up!"

"See you tomorrow."

"Okay."

And we meet the next day at three o'clock and fight all over again, same rules. Then we do it again the day after that. You can set your clock by my fights.

*   *   *

In junior high, I have my first direct encounter with an angry black man. In this case, an angry black kid.

One morning, a minute before eight, I slide into my seat in homeroom and start unpacking my books. Two rows away, a guy I ride the bus with, a guy I've known for years—Brandon, a feared bully, a large, hulking kid with a permanent scowl and premature mustache—leans over to me and growls, "Yo. I'm kicking your ass. You know that. Today. Lunch, boy!"

I look at him, unsure I've heard him right. "Fuck, Brandon."

Brandon nods. "That's right. I'm busting your ass."

Brandon is tough. A serious hard-ass. Brandon could do me some major harm. Brandon has *Future Criminal and Prison Inmate* already tattooed on his forehead. I let out a nervous laugh.

"Fuck, man."

Brandon sears me with a stare. "Don't laugh, boy. You go ahead and laugh and giggle and all that. I'm serious. I am busting your ass."

I shake my head. "Why do you wanna do that?"

He shrugs. "Just do."

So this is how my day starts. And this is how it goes. Every period, every class Brandon slowly walks down the aisle, sits down at his desk, overwhelming his tiny, too-small chair, stretches over to me, and says, "Lunchtime, boy. I'm busting your ass."

I watch the clock like I'm the victim in *High Noon*. The minutes tick by. At the start of every class, Brandon leans over and whispers, "You know I ain't forgot. Naw. I'm busting your ass."

I can't focus on anything the teachers say. All the subjects run together—history, math, science, English. Nothing makes sense. All I'm able to do is run lunchtime scenarios over in my mind, all involving me, an ambulance, and paramedics. Doomsday is coming early to Detroit. The Apocalypse is now. At least mine is. I start mumbling aloud, over and over, "Got-damn. What do I do?"

Last period before lunch. My hands are clammy and cold. The blackboard looks out of focus and blurry. I think about writing out a will.

Then it hits me. Very simply.

What the fuck?

I know exactly what I'm gonna do. It's bold. Crazy. And possibly suicidal. But I'm gonna do it anyway.

Brandon, cracking his knuckles the way all bullies do, because apparently bullies have extra-huge knuckles designed for smashing in faces, lurches down the aisle toward his desk. He bangs into my shoulder on purpose. Stops. Glares at me.

"Forty-five minutes, boy. Then I am busting your ass."

I look him straight in the eye.

"Why?"

Brandon's bottom lip rolls out. Quivers in either rage or confusion.

"What?"

"*Why?*" I say with urgency.

Brandon lays a heavy, massive paw on my desk.

"Listen—"

"No," I say quietly, my eyes still locked on his. "You listen, Brandon. I'm not gonna fight you."

"Oh, you are gonna fight."

"No, I'm not. I'm not gonna fight you. You know why?"

He doesn't answer. His eyes widen.

"Because you're my friend," I say.

Brandon's mouth opens, closes, opens again. He starts to speak, breaks my stare, studies the ceiling. He takes a deep breath, then moves his paw in a circle on my desk. I stare at his oversized and gnarly fingers, expecting them to lift and circle my throat.

"All right," he says, sniffing. Now I'm expecting him to spit. Instead he looks past me, apparently finding something fascinating on the map of the United States that's spread open across the entire far wall.

"You got away," he says, and then repeats the words, more for himself than for me. "You got away."

He stands at my desk for what feels like a month, then slowly—painfully slowly—finds his desk and crashes into his chair.

I let out enough air to start up a windmill.

Then I silently whisper a prayer of thanks to God, or to whatever angel stood watch over me and saved me from getting my ass kicked by Brandon. Because if saying I wasn't going to fight him didn't work, other than begging for my life, I had no other ideas.

I guess it's obvious by now. I'm not cut out to be a violent angry young black man. I'm certainly not cut out to be much of a fighter. I lack the natural killer instinct.

Case in point.

Every day on the bus a kid in my grade named Sidney taunts me. He's ruthless and relentless. He makes fun of my name, my size, my nose, eyes, ears, mouth, and forehead. He laughs at the way I walk, the way I talk, the way my voice sounds. He then works his way into my relationships. He rags on my friends and dumps on my brother and sister, even though he's never met them. Hell, he's never *seen* them. He stops short of bagging on my parents because he knows they're off limits, but I can tell he's tempted.

The reason I don't put my fist in Sidney's eye is that Sidney is half my size.

He knows this gives him a huge advantage over me. And he flaunts it.

One day, I can't take it anymore. When the bus pulls over to let some kids off, I shoot out of my seat and get into Sidney's face.

"Sidney, I'm warning you! Shut the fuck up!"

"Or what? What you gonna do?"

He stands up. Damn. The bitch barely comes up to my waist. I can't hit him. First, I'll feel terrible. Like pounding on a midget. Or a girl in the third grade. Second, everybody in the whole school will be on my case. I'll never live it down.

The doors hiss shut and the bus lurches forward.

"Or *what?*" Sidney repeats in his annoying, fucked-up, high-pitched, singsong, twinkle-ass Looney Toons voice. "Huh? What you gonna do, Guh-rear-end?"

I don't know why that riles me up. Sidney has said a lot worse shit to me, but that just sends me over the edge.

I shove him back into his seat.

At that moment, the bus stops short.

Sidney sails out of his seat like he's been shot out of a cannon, flies through the air, hits the slick green patch of linoleum that stretches down the center of the bus, and rolls all the way down the aisle, as if I have bowled him. He rolls into the driver's ticket-collecting column and stops with a clunk. After a two-second delay, he melts into the floor.

I charge him. Sidney tries to make a run for it, but there is nowhere to go. I reach my arms out to grab him, preferably by the throat. He ducks under me and tries to make it to the other end of the bus. I grab the back of his shirt and pull him toward me.

"This is not over, Sidney," I say, doing my best Brandon-the-bully impression. "We're gonna keep going."

Sidney tries to speak but can't. His lips suddenly look caked and dry.

I pull him close. Face-to-face.

"Get off at the next stop, motherfucker, or I'm gonna bust your ass right here. You understand?"

Sidney manages a nod.

I drop him like the sack of shit he is, waggle my finger into his face, a final punctuation point, and press myself against the rear bus doors. I crane my neck and see that the bus is approaching the next stop. I nod at Sidney. I make a fist and punch my palm. Nice touch, I think. I've seen Brandon do that a couple of times. Works for him.

The bus screeches to a stop.

"Get off here, Sid-ney," I say in what I imagine to be a terrifying voice.

I step forward as the bus doors behind me open. Very coolly, I step backwards off the bus. I have never felt so strong. If there is one time in my life where I'm actually in the mood to kick some serious ass, this is it. I am so ready. I am going to fucking bury this punk. I want to teach him a lesson he will never forget. I'm gonna rearrange the features on his fucking ugly little gnome of a face. I am gonna nip and tuck his sorry ass using my fist as a scalpel. I'm gonna move his mouth up to where his eyes are, yank off the little fucker's nose and stick it into one of his ears, then tear off both of his ears and shove them into his mouth, then I'm gonna stomp—

The bus takes off.

Sidney sits at the back window, his face smooshed against it. He waves, then gives me the finger.

"Hey!" I scream. "You little asshole! Come back here! HEY!!!"

I race after the bus. The bus pulls away, turns the corner, and is gone. I stand on the sidewalk like an idiot, watching Sidney escape.

Note to self. If you're gonna beat somebody up, make sure you got the somebody there with you. It helps.

7

HOUSE BURNING DOWN

I have now become a Black Panther. One afternoon, dressed in a black leather jacket, black beret, and sunglasses, I discuss the fine points of the cause with my best friend, Richard Wilson.

"The proletariat is denigrating the whole oppressed minority," I say to Richard, who's also wearing a black leather jacket, black beret, and sunglasses.

"Exactly. It's about getting the Man's attention," Richard says.

I shake my head. "Nonviolence has not worked, Richard. We have to do more than talk. It's all in here."

I hand Richard my dog-eared paperback copy of Eldridge

✳ 81 ✳

Cleaver's *Soul on Ice,* the bible of the movement. Richard takes it from me, pores over the back flap copy.

"You wanna get something to eat?" he says.

"Sure."

"I don't feel like going out. You got anything in your fridge?"

Okay. Truth. I am fifteen. Richard and I are in my room. And I am not a Black Panther . . . yet. The Panthers, the organization begun by Bobby Seale and Huey Newton, is made up of scores of sexy, strong, angry young black men. They are rock stars. I can tell that they are respected politically and that they get plenty of pussy. Which is one key reason I want to be one of them.

"We should go there," Richard says.

"Where?"

"Black Panther headquarters." Richard speaks as casually as if he were suggesting going to a Tigers game.

"What are you talking about?"

I'm intrigued and just a little bit scared.

Richard shrugs. "I know where it is. It's not that far. It's on Philadelphia and Lynwood."

"You mean just go over there and join?"

"Yeah. 'Course I should probably read the book first."

"I like this idea. Volunteer for the cause."

"Unless you don't want to," Richard says.

"I want to. Do you?"

"You know I do."

Neither of us does.

But neither of us is going to back down now.

✶　✶　✶

One day, the following week after school, dressed in army jackets and sunglasses, Richard and I make our way to Philadelphia Avenue. We turn up the street, pass a few houses, and stop. In the middle of the block sits a two-story brick house. Most of the windows are boarded up. A poster with a Black Power fist is slapped onto the front door, which is riddled with bullet holes.

"I think we found it," Richard says.

"You think? Really?"

Neither of us moves.

"What should we do?" Richard says.

"We could knock on the door."

"I guess."

"That's why we're here, right?"

"Yeah."

We still don't move.

"I'm going in," I say.

I take two steps toward the front door, which flies open with a jolt, scaring the shit out of me. A thin young man in his twenties wearing a black leather jacket, wraparound sunglasses, and a black beret stands in the doorway.

"All power to the people," he says. Somehow he speaks without making his lips move.

"All power to the people," Richard and I say in unison.

"What do you want?"

"We want to join up," I say. "You don't have to pay us or anything. We want to enlist. As volunteers."

Behind me, Richard nods enthusiastically. He has suddenly become a mute.

"Uh-huh. So you want to join us, my brothers?"

"Yes, sir."

"Are you ready to assume your role in the cause of the revolution? Are you prepared to sacrifice your life, if need be, to get the attention of the Man?"

"Oh, yes. Well, I mean. My life. That's a big—"

The young man in leather flips down his sunglasses and peeks at us as if seeing us for the first time.

"How old are you?"

"Fifteen," I say. "And a half."

He sniffs. "You're too young. Too young to join the struggle. We don't take anyone under sixteen."

I'm suddenly both indignant and relieved.

"We're too young to join the *struggle*? Did you hear that, Richard? We didn't make the cutoff."

I turn around. Richard is halfway up the street. He waves and keeps going.

I turn back toward the Panther in the leather jacket.

"Darn," I say, feeling a sudden wave of real disappointment.

"Come back when you turn sixteen," the young man says, pulling the door closed.

Damn. How will I get pussy now?

＊　＊　＊

A month later.

I am no longer a Black Panther. I no longer dress from head to toe in black. I no longer recite whole passages from *Soul on Ice* aloud from memory.

I realize that being a Black Panther is not who I am. I was going through a phase. I became enamored of the Black Panther persona. Taken in by the politics. I see that now. I decide not to join the revolution. I am going to hold off participating in the struggle. Besides, my mother won't let me.

I don't know how she finds out about our visit to Philadelphia Avenue and Black Panther headquarters. I suspect Richard. I have no hard evidence, but I'm fairly certain he cracked under heavy interrogation while eating something delicious that my mother baked, maybe especially for him.

When she finds out, she flips. She explains that the Panthers are targeted by the FBI. She's heard that the Feds or people acting as the Feds routinely drag young black men out of that house and make them disappear. She forbids me to go back there.

It's just as well. I see that becoming a Black Panther was ridiculous, childish, impossible, even laughable. I'm not sure what I was thinking. I have matured. I have moved on.

Yes, I am no longer a Black Panther.

I am now Jimi Hendrix.

To be honest, I am not just Jimi Hendrix.

I am also his guitar.

I have memorized not only all the lyrics to all the songs on all of his three albums, I have also memorized—and imitate—all of his guitar solos in all the songs on all of his three albums. With my voice. In my head, Jimi's guitar playing and my imitation of his guitar playing sound almost identical. Of course, I have my favorites. I am obsessed with all his albums, but I experience something close to a divine connection to *Electric Ladyland,* his third and most recent album. I do uncanny imitations of the guitar solo openings to

"Crosstown Traffic" and "Voodoo Chile," but I consider the thirty-second thunderous *wa-weh-weh-wah* beginning to "Burning of the Midnight Lamp" my masterpiece.

The fact is there is no one like Jimi Hendrix. I idolize him. He is The One. He is the baddest motherfucker in the world. And he is black. There is no better combination. The angry black man lives!

I imitate his walk. I imitate his low-voiced, indifferent, near mumble. And of course I imitate his style.

Or try to. I pore through rock 'n' roll magazines and cut out Jimi's pictures and paste them up in my room. I ask my mother to take me shopping for clothes. She regards me with suspicion. It is highly unusual for fifteen-year-old boys to ask their moms to take them shopping for clothes.

"You want to buy new clothes?" she asks. "What for?"

"I don't know. I want to change how I look."

"What's wrong with the way you look? What do you want to look like?"

"I saw these silver boots with rainbows on them in a magazine. I really want to get a pair."

"Why would you want to wear silver boots with rainbows?"

"I also want purple velvet pants."

My mother stares at me. "David, I'm very worried about you right now. I'm very worried that you are interested in wearing silver boots with rainbows and velvet pants."

"And medallions around my neck. Lots of medallions and chains. I'm going to be wearing a neon orange-sunset-bursting tie-dyed shirt and I'm going to be wearing it open—"

In the end she never buys me silver boots with rainbows or purple velvet pants or medallions. I get as far as wearing a bright pink headband one day to metal shop class. My shop teacher, Mr. Jenkins, stops me on my way in.

"What is that?"

"What?"

"On your head."

"It's a headband."

"Take that got-damn thing off. You look like a fruit. Give it to me. I'm gonna use it for a rag to wipe the grease off the drill press. Or to wipe my nose. Get into class!"

I pull off my headband, stuff it in my pocket, and, taking my time, stride into the metal shop, slowwwly, the way I imagine Jimi would.

I'm unfazed. Nothing my mother says, or Mr. Jenkins says, or anyone else says, matters. I *am* Jimi Hendrix, and even though I'm only in high school, I am, in my mind, a rock star and angry black man, the coolest one-two punch in the world.

☀ ☀ ☀

November 30, 1968.

At the time, in my life, this is merely the most important day in the history of the world. On this day, Jimi Hendrix is playing for one night only at Cobo Hall in Detroit and I'm going. My brother, Geoffrey, by far the most wonderful brother in the world—no, the *universe*—has bought a block of tickets to the concert and has invited me and a friend to go with him. Geoffrey has become active in our church's youth group, and in a show of social cross-pollination and ethnic solidarity, has volunteered to take ten kids from his group and another ten from an all-white youth group to attend the concert.

"I got two tickets for you, too," he says. "Pick you up after school. Be in the driveway, because I want to get downtown early."

I can barely contain myself. Can't sleep the night before. Spend an hour choosing my wardrobe. I don't want to show up at the concert looking too much like Jimi. What if he sees me and he finds my outfit offensive? But maybe he'll be flattered. I compromise, wear my headband, and decide to save my tie-dyed T-shirt for school the next day when I can brag to everyone that I was there.

By the way, I can trace my obsession for dressing up like rock stars to the arrival of The Beatles several years earlier when I was eight years old. Like every rock 'n' roll crazed kid in America, I went nuts over The Beatles. And like every rock 'n' roll crazed kid in America, I wanted to wear my hair in a Beatles haircut. Easy. All it took was a little ingenuity and creativity.

When my mother washed my father's clothes, she would gather all of his black and brown knee-high dress socks and tie them together in a bundle. *Bam.* Perfect Beatles wig. I would lay my dad's dress sock bundle on my head, use a broom as a guitar, and rock out in the mirror to "Ticket to Ride." Didn't everybody?

The day of the concert, Richard—my choice to see Jimi—and I don't walk home from school; we run. As we jog, we argue over which song Jimi will play first. He's on his *Electric Ladyland* tour, so we know he'll be doing most of, if not all, the songs from that album. We laugh about the two dorks we overheard yesterday in the park arguing over the correct way to pronounce *chile* in the song "Voodoo Chile" from the album.

"It's chile, like, 'Get in the house, chile,'" dork one says.

"No, it's chile, like, 'Man, I just ate some spicy chile,'" dork two says.

They argue, then agree. It's the second way. What dorks!

Laughing, Richard and I arrive in my driveway out of breath both from sprinting the last block and from excitement and anticipation.

As it turns out, we could've walked to my house.

Hell, we could've crawled.

My brother never shows.

I'm way beyond pissed. And not just because I didn't see Jimi Hendrix perform. I'm beyond pissed because my brother *met* Jimi Hendrix.

Here's what happens. Supposedly.

The reason Geoffrey leaves us stranded in the driveway is that he doesn't have any money left to buy our tickets. He buys the tickets to cover the two youth groups, but instead of buying two more tickets for me and Richard, he buys liquor and weed. Incredibly thoughtless. What's even more thoughtless is that he spends *all* his money on liquor and weed and forgets to leave anything left over to purchase tickets for himself and his friend.

He makes sure the other youth group members get their tickets, then, broke, dejected, ticket-less, and stoned, he and his friend circle around to the back of Cobo Hall hoping that they can somehow sneak into the concert.

All of a sudden, a long black limo pulls up and screeches to a stop. The doors fly open, and, unbelievably, Jimi Hendrix steps out of the backseat. He's late, he's in a rush, but walking coolly, calmly, as if he's got all the time in the world. He starts heading into the artists' entrance of the theater. As if pulled by a pied piper, my brother and his friend follow behind, get in step with him. Nobody questions them as they go with Jimi inside Cobo Hall and continue into Jimi's dressing room. It's as if they're part of Jimi's entourage. At one point, Jimi turns to my brother and stares at him.

"I'm busted," Geoffrey thinks.

"You guys want anything?" Jimi asks him.

Stunned, my brother politely refuses but somehow manages to explain that they don't have tickets to the show. Jimi nods at Noel Redding, one of the band members, and before they know it, Noel leads them through a maze of hallways backstage, then across the stage, and into two seats a few rows from the front of the stage.

So, while I wait all afternoon and into the night for my brother to show, he has not only gotten into the concert for free but he has also met Jimi Hendrix and hung out with him in his dressing room before the show.

I still have not forgiven him.

✻　✻　✻

There is one slight problem with being Jimi Hendrix.

All my friends know about and tolerate my Jimi obsession (hell, most of them dig him, too), but other kids, mainly larger and older kids—those who don't know me well and who like to kick my ass for sport—are not aware that I am angry and bad, the junior high version of Hendrix.

Partly this is because I play the cello.

Not my choice. The school's suggestion, which my mother endorses.

"The cello is a beautiful instrument, David."

"No, it's not. It's big and bulky and weird and I hate it."

"Try it. You might change your mind."

Since the school has provided me with a free cello and lessons during lunch, I can't say no. I promise my mother I'll give it a month.

The first week, I lug the cello with me onto the bus. I accidentally wham two kids sitting in the front. They slap and punch me as I drag the thing through the bus to the back, where I squeeze by two other kids who I can tell are getting into the mood to kick my ass. Except that kicking my ass alone wouldn't be any fun.

"Is that your fucking cello?"

"No. It belongs to the school."

"You get in trouble if you don't bring it back in one piece?"

I know where this is going. I shrug, as if I don't know or don't care.

"Oh yeah. You gonna get in trouble."

So fun for them would be playing keep-away, and *then* kicking my ass. Which they do.

You'd figure that after hassling me about my cello and kicking my ass, these larger and older kids, probably eighth graders, would be done with me after a day or two. Three at most.

You would be wrong.

Every day for two weeks, the same kids play the same stupid game of keep-away with me, before kicking my ass. I wish I could run away from them. But I can't. First, you can't run with a cello. It kinda slows you down. Second, the stupid cello isn't even mine. It belongs to the school. I can't drop and leave the stupid cello on the bus or out on the street, especially one that belongs to the school. The school would then kick my ass. And then after my mom finds out, she'll kick my ass. Then she'll call my dad in San Francisco and the next time he sees me, he'll really kick my ass. So I have no choice but to take the daily ass kickings from the kids on the bus.

Finally, on the fifteenth day, they get bored and stop. I am let off the hook at last. Or so I think.

Wrong again.

A fat chick who's been giving me the moldy stink eye for two weeks waddles over, wrestles the cello away from me, and sits on it. Beneath her rump, I hear the sound of wood snapping and air escaping, which I assume is coming from the cello but could be coming from the fat chick.

"Ah," she says, glaring at me. "I need to sit down."

She wriggles her ass. More wood splintering. More air escaping.

The next day I return the cello to the band teacher.

"I'm giving up the cello," I say. "Before it kills me."

✳   ✳   ✳

At some point between my Black Panther stage and my Jimi Hendrix stage, I set our house on fire. Even though there is a song on *Electric Ladyland* called "House Burning Down," I'm pretty sure there's no connection.

The night I set our house on fire is set in my memory like a dream. Images, sounds, even colors have blended together over time. I'm not even sure exactly how old I am. I do know that it is Thanksgiving evening at our house. We've finished our seemingly endless turkey dinner, which started at two in the afternoon. The house is full of people—family, friends, neighbors—most of whom are lying around the living room and dining room, spilling onto our staircase and landing, telling stories, laughing, gossiping, full and lazy after dinner.

Not interested in hanging with the adults, we kids fend for ourselves. My brother and his friends ignore me, I don't care what my sister and her friends are up to, and I just want to go down to the basement and play with matches.

Like a lot of my friends, I'm fascinated by fire. I'm not an arsonist or anything. I just like to set things on fire and watch them burst into flame.

Goes back to when I was a little kid. Always loved to play with fireworks. I was partial to Roman candles, the ones that shot up, popped, sizzled, and came right back at you so you'd have to jump out of the way or have your clothes or hair catch on fire.

Best of all, I loved making plastic models of cars, airplanes, and warships and blowing them up. The trick to a good explosion is to insert the firecracker *inside* the model, then build the model around the incendiary device. If you're really ambitious or artistic, you can go all the way and slap on the decals that come with the kit, even paint the fucking thing and then blow it up. Gives it a more realistic and spectacular effect.

By the way, lighting the firecracker's fuse and running like hell is old school when it comes to blowing up your model. Nothing wrong with it. Just boring. A better way is to light your models on fire and shove them out of your bedroom window. This is great, especially if your bedroom is on the second floor. The caution here is to make sure your flaming PT boat or burning B-52 doesn't explode all over your dad's new car or land in the clothes in your mom's laundry basket, causing all of the family's bedding, towels, and underwear to incinerate.

I hesitate to reveal the following unsavory moment from my past on the off chance that someone from Homeland Security is reading this and is going to turn me in. What the hell. I'll take my chances.

I made a bomb. That's not true.

I made several bombs.

We all did. That's what little boys do. Well, maybe not all little boys, but all the little boys I knew. We liked to make rockets and bombs and explode stuff. We even once tried to make chlorine gas. We couldn't get it to work. The gas was supposed to have had a green glow. We couldn't get past a sludgy brown goo. As we were swirling the liquid around, one of my friends said, "Isn't this, like, gonna kill us?" I grunted, shrugged. We didn't really think that far ahead.

It's so easy to make a bomb that it's almost criminal.

All you need are a box of firecrackers and a few other common items you're sure to have around the house.

Since we lived so close to Canada, where fireworks are legal, we always kept a stash of firecrackers in our basement. Boxes of them. We had a regular cache. Shit, we had a militia down there. Of course, my mom didn't know. Why tell her? She had so much on her mind.

When I was really little, my brother showed me how to make my first bomb. If I'm going down, Geoffrey, you're coming with me. I don't know who in my family long ago was blessed with the munitions-expert-blow-your-ass-up gene, but my brother inherited it. He had some skills. He taught me everything I know.

First, we took apart a box of firecrackers. We then poured out all the gunpowder and packed it into a glass jar. No special glass jar. Just a regular glass jar everyone has lying around the house. An empty jam jar or peanut butter jar, for instance, will do fine. You add a waterproof fuse, some ball bearings, and, boom, blow the mother-fucker up.

Now, I'm only a kid, but I'm no fool. I'm not going to explode my first bomb in our backyard. No way. I explode that bomb far away from our house so there is no chance my mom will hear it. I go two full houses away. Almost to the corner. I set it off early in the morning, too. When nobody's up. About nine o'clock. Cover all my bases.

The noise from that bomb going off is ear-shattering. A cannon blast. A sonic boom. I am unprepared for the sheer volume of the explosion. It is thrilling. And frightening. And fucking LOUD.

I race home so I will not be found out.

My mother is waiting for me outside.

"What was that?"

I look her right in the eye. I am so cool. So smooth. So good at lying.

"I'm—not—ah, you know, what are you, ha, talking about?"

She opens her hand. She is holding a box of firecrackers.

I blink at them.

I go for total stupidity here. It's my only chance. Frankly, sounding and looking like a total idiot has worked well for me in the past.

"Wow. What are those?"

"Get in the house. I'm calling your father."

I am so busted.

*   *   *

I am pretty much over my pyro stage when I set the house on fire that Thanksgiving. I'm no longer into making bombs, blowing up model airplanes, and trying to manufacture lethal gas. At least not on any regular basis. I'm just a typical red-blooded American boy into fire games in the basement, such as "fire tag," which you play with a friend and a box of lit wooden matches. Simple rules. Whoever's "it" tosses lit matches at the other guy. Soon as you catch the victim with your match, you switch. Clothes count. Causing the other person's hair to smoke counts double. It's way fun. You definitely see and receive your share of sparks, but don't worry, actual instances of setting the other person on fire are rare.

When we play—and frankly, we don't play that often—we never bother to take into account the fact that our house is old. Not exactly in disrepair, but like most old houses, it could benefit from an upgrade in certain areas like plumbing, painting, heating, and wiring. There is no rush, and certainly no danger. We've had the same wiring for seventy-five years. Endured seventy-five brutal Detroit winters and oppressive summers. Never an incident.

Running through the basement, dodging behind four-foot-tall mummy-wrapped piles of freaky-looking weird cake-batter-type shit, which, in retrospect, were probably bolts of asbestos, we brush past a few loose wires hanging down. Nothing unusual or out of place about that. We are, after all, in the basement. Lotta strange shit down here. And the wires aren't frayed, or twitching, or sparking. They've just managed to pop out from their corset of staples and are now dangling from the low ceiling like tentacles from some hidden, space-age squid. We never give the wires a second thought.

That Thanksgiving, I'm recalling the highlights of a season of fire tag while I absently strike kitchen matches from a box I snatched upstairs. The key to playing with fire, of course, is to approximate danger without ever actually coming anywhere near danger. In this case, I've found an area of the basement where a small flap of insulation paper pokes out from the wall like a sail. I flick the insulation with my finger. Probably left over from an unfinished basement remodel, I figure, as I light the bottom of the insulation with a match, allow it to flare, and prepare to blow out the flame, as I've just done twenty or thirty straight times. This time, though, the tiny blue flame cartwheels up the insulation paper and nips the bottom of a dangling wire that hangs over my shoulder.

The wire jerks as if coming to life, sputters, crackles, and bursts into flame. The flashing burning wire shimmies like a snake and flicks against the far wall. *Baroosh.* A small fire erupts. Blue flames lick the baseboard.

"Shit," I say and instinctively race upstairs. I careen around the kitchen, slide into the dining room, fly through a pocket of guests, and find my mother, who is sipping coffee at the table, holding court.

"The house is on fire!" I whisper frantically.

"What?"

"I was in the basement and these wires were hanging, and—"

That's all I get out. My mother leaps for the phone and calls 911, while a handful of adults head into the cellar. Another group gathers the rest of the people inside the house and herds them outside onto the lawn. Within minutes, the fire department arrives. Two burly firefighters dressed in crinkly yellow slickers and hard yellow fire hats—the kind of hat I've always wanted—rush into the house and charge into the basement, sending the handful of adults back up the stairs. From down below, after only a minute or so, a voice shouts up, "All clear," and the two firefighters climb into the kitchen to a communal hissing of relief and actual applause. A few of the guests clap me on the back. I'm a hero. I've saved the day.

"Is everything okay?" my mother asks the firefighters.

"It's out," one of them says. "Hadn't built to much." He removes his hat, rubs a darkened fist along his cheek, scratches his head.

"Must have been a short," one of the adults near me says. I try not to agree too enthusiastically.

"I think you should see this," the firefighter says to my mom, indicating the cellar stairs. She hesitates.

"After you," he says. My mother disappears into the basement. The firefighter lowers his head—either from his height or shyness—and starts down after her. I'm not sure I hear correctly, but I think his muffled voice floats back up to the kitchen, right where I'm standing, and he's asking, "Do you have kids?"

*   *   *

Later, my mother gathers my brother, sister, and me into the dining room and repeats the conversation she and the firefighter had in the basement.

"This house is old," the firefighter said. "But solid as a rock. They don't make 'em like this anymore."

"Meaning?"

"Nothing's wrong with the wiring. No reason the wiring would short out and ignite by itself. Can't happen."

"Let me understand. What you're saying is, the fire was set?"

"Yes, ma'am."

"Are you sure?"

"A hundred percent."

*   *   *

That night, I barely sleep. I wake up in a pool of sweat knowing that I have to confess.

I don't expect the confession to be a two-parter. I do expect the confession to go badly, since my mother has already asked me point-blank, "David, did you set the fire?" and I have already said, "Me? Are you kidding? No. I found the fire. Set the fire? Man."

I know what I have to do. I just want to get it over with, take my punishment, and get on with my life, such as it is. Shaking like a leaf, on the verge of tears, legs heavy, I stumble into my mom's bedroom. I must look like shit, because she raises her head, her eyes cloud, and she says, with alarm in her voice, "David, what's the matter?"

Voice shaking, I somehow manage to force the words out. And as I confess to setting the fire, a surprising feeling of relief weighing about as much as a car lifts off me. I feel lighter. The burden I've been carrying floats away.

"I'm glad you found the courage to tell me," my mother says.

"Oh, me, too," and then I add, "I'm so sorry. I promise I will never, ever, EVER, do anything like that again. I swear on my life!"

"That's good, David. I believe you. Now, we'll just have to decide on an appropriate punishment."

"I completely understand. But as you're deciding on my punishment, and I agree that I deserve something harsh, though not too harsh, since I am a child, and as a child, I learn from my mistakes, I ask that you consider not only my age but the fact that I did come to you on my own—"

I stop. My brain flashes back to a word my mother said, one word that stands out, as if underlined in red.

I swallow. "What do you mean . . . *we*?"

"We," my mother says, "meaning myself and your father."

＊　＊　＊

I hadn't counted on this.

Had not counted on my father being part of the equation. Hadn't thought that he'd be one of those deciding my fate. Even worse, I hadn't counted on my mother turning the whole affair over to him.

Because two weeks after I start the fire, I'm sent to San Francisco for a visit with my dad.

Psychiatrists are big on confronting issues, dealing with feelings, facing your fears, all that kind of shit. It happens this quickly. Walking into his apartment, helping me in with my suitcase, my father brings up the "issue" almost before I have my coat off.

"So," he says, "let's get it out in the open, David."

"Okay," I say.

"Your mother told me that one of you kids set the house on fire."

I look him directly in the eye, wearing my most incredulous look, a look I've practiced for hours on the plane.

"She told you *what*?"

"She said you set the house on fire."

I allow my mouth to drop open. All part of my plan. Keep my eyes locked on his. "Set the—why would I do that?"

He blinks. Actually flinches. I go now for my second look, a combination of shock, disbelief, and hurt. Tough to pull off, I know. But this one I got down.

"Well, did you?" my father says.

"Hell, no."

My father mumbles something under his breath. I think I pick up the words "Woman's crazy, always trying to start some shit," then he claps his hands and says, "Hey, you hungry? You want to order in some Chinese?"

"Sounds great," I say, while inside, a chorus is clapping, raising their arms to the heavens, singing, shouting, "Free at last, free at last, free at last!"

*   *   *

P.S.

A casting director's office. Twenty-five years later.

I am auditioning for a part in a movie about a kid who sets his house on fire.

Among my competition is Sinbad, the comic, a friend. We share a battered leather couch, waiting to be called in to read for the producers. Flipping through the script, I say, as casually as I can, "I may have an advantage on you."

"Oh, really? Why's that?"

I chuckle. "Well, when I was a kid, I actually did set my house on fire."

"Is that right?"

"True."

Sinbad tilts his head toward me and lifts an eyebrow. "DAG, *every* black comic set the house on fire. I set my house on fire. Everybody I *know* set their house on fire. Shit."

My confidence leaves. Exits stage left.

"Oh. Okay. I didn't realize—"

I don't get the gig.

* * * **8** * * *

PURPLE HAZE

November 6, 2008.

The morning after the election.

I wake to blades of sunlight stabbing me through the blinds and an empty bed. I stretch over and squint at the alarm.

Is that right? Almost *noon*? Can't be right. We must have had a power outage or something. My head is pounding. I feel hungover but I know I didn't drink last night. I swirled a couple swallows of champagne before I got up onstage, but that was it.

Man. That party. Wall-to-wall people. Over-the-edge emotion.

Ten thousand more celebrants outside the hotel partying on the street. It's all coming back to me now. The Hyatt Regency in Century City, hosting the Democratic election night party. I use the word "host" loosely. Nothing like standing in front of 1,500 strangers and having an emotional breakdown. Crying hysterically. The crowd urging me on.

"Let it go, DAG, it's all right, let it go!"

I shudder.

Well, at least this is now true:

Barack Obama is officially President-elect Barack Obama.

That alone propels me out of bed.

I shower, dress, and find my way to the kitchen. Christine is puttering around, Luisa slung over her shoulder. I kiss them both. I pick up a warm glow. It feels like a new day.

"So," Christine says, offering up a shy smile, which means there is something on her mind, usually something that she wants me to do. "Did you mean what you said last night?"

"I said a lot of things last night. Most of which I did not mean. What are you referring to?"

"The inauguration. Do you really think you can get us tickets?"

Now, I know she is asking an innocent question. But I take her question as a challenge. And, in fact, I really do want to go to the inauguration.

"Hell, yes."

"You really think you can?"

"What did I just say? Wait. Let me rephrase this. No, I don't think I can get us tickets. I *know* I can get us tickets. I'm on it."

I start fixing myself breakfast. I'm quiet now, a silent man, leaning just a tad toward intense. Because in my head I'm planning out my moves.

Okay, truth.

I have no moves. Have no idea how to get tickets to the inauguration. Have no idea where to start.

"I gotta make a call," I say finally.

"Who you gonna call?"

"Don't worry. I got it covered. I know exactly who I'm gonna call for the tickets. My ticket guy."

"You have a ticket guy?"

"Oh, yes. Didn't I tell you about him? Mr. Tickets. Donald Ducats. He always comes through. Get you tickets to anything. Gonna call him right now."

I go into my office and call everybody I know. I call all the producers on *Chocolate News,* one of whom sends me over to someone at the network, who sends me back to someone on the show, who sends me to someone in public relations, who tells me her assistant is handling inauguration ticket requests, who puts me on hold, and then hangs up on me. I call back, get a busy signal, call again and get voice mail, leave a frantic message, call a friend to vent, who listens sympathetically, picks up his call waiting, comes back, tells me he has to take this call because it's about his getting TICKETS TO THE INAUGURATION.

Christine comes into my office. She brings me a cup of coffee, gently puts it on my desk. "How's it going?"

"Well," I say. "Very well."

"Any luck?"

"Yes. Oh, yes. It looks good. Excellent."

I sip my coffee. She nods, smiles, kisses my forehead.

"There is no ticket guy, is there?"

"Uh, okay, no."

She rubs my back in a circle.

"I know you're still going to get the tickets," she says as she leaves. "I have confidence in you."

That is about the worst thing she could say.

Now I really, *really* have to get those tickets to the inauguration.

I start over. I call the network person back. I argue how *Chocolate News* has been a champion of Barack Obama. I stress that in the vast landscape of televised political punditry—almost all of it *white*—we have been one of the only outlets for the black perspective. Did someone just play the Race Card? Yes. I did. Not to mention that we're edgy and satiric. I become insistent, start to get angry, and then, okay, I beg. A little plea, that's all. It works. After a moment of dead air, the network person tells me to call a woman named Janet, who has the fishy title of "liaison," which I hope is French for "I can get you tickets."

I call Janet. On her voice mail I leave my name, number, request for tickets, and a sense of urgency. I slump back into my chair and rub the bridge of my nose with my thumbs. If worse comes to worst, we'll just crash the inauguration. We'll go to the National Mall at night. We'll wear camouflage and smear black shoe polish under our eyes. What that does, I have no idea, but if it'll help hide us, we're gonna do it. Then I'll give Christine a boost, put my weight under her, and shove her over the fence, then climb over myself.

Who am I kidding?

I am a fifty-two-year-old comedian and host of a fake news show on Comedy Central. I'm not an ex–CIA commando. I sing, I dance, I tell dick jokes. I don't climb fences.

I'm doomed. My wife is gonna lose confidence in me. . . .

I'm not even sure what that means anymore. I just know it's not good.

The phone rings.

I grab it, nearly shout hello.

Janet. A quick introduction, couple of pleasantries.

"Janet, I know you're hearing this a lot today," I say, "but I need tickets to the inauguration."

"Yeah, I have heard that once or twice," she says.

She is sweet and cool. Beyond that. Her voice and manner are soothing. Comforting.

"Is there anything you can do?" I ask.

"We're working on it," she says.

At the moment, those are the most beautiful words in the English language.

We're working on it.

"Really?" I say.

"Don't get excited," she says. "Yet."

"Yet," I say.

"I'll get back to you," Janet says.

She hangs up. I putter around for the next hour or so. Play with Luisa. Take her for a walk. Work out. Push around some papers on my desk. Check e-mails. Answer a few. Kill some spam.

The phone rings. I check the time. Two hours after my call with Janet.

"Update," Janet says.

"Yes?"

I cannot conceal my anticipation, my nervousness, my *hope*.

"I'm working on the tickets," she says. "Working it hard."

"And?"

Slight pause.

"I think we can pull something off," Janet says.

"Yes!"

"I think so."

"Look, Janet, I don't care where I sit. I don't even have to sit, I'll stand. I don't care if I'm in the back row. I don't care if I'm the last one in. I just need tickets to this inauguration."

"Let me see what I can do."

"Not to be pushy or anything, but should I make my plane and hotel reservations?"

"You haven't done that? Yes. Absolutely. Do that immediately."

"So you're pretty sure you can get the tickets?"

"Working on it," she says and hangs up.

I make the plane reservations. This is before the economy goes into flush mode and airlines are practically paying you to fly. This is when the airlines are flying high, charging an arm and a leg. And finding a hotel that week in Washington, D.C.? Wow. Like trying to get seats on the fifty-yard line at the Super Bowl. Of course, bottom line: if you're willing to pay, you can buy almost anything. That is the American way.

Well, this is the inauguration of President Barack Obama. I am willing to pay. So I do. A fucking fortune.

Janet better come through with those tickets.

✹ ✹ ✹

Janet comes through with the tickets.

But it takes her forever. Days go by. A week. Finally, she calls late one afternoon.

"DAG?"

"Janet!"

She sighs, deeply. For a second, I fear the worst.

"You're not going to believe this."

"Believe what? Oh, no. Don't tell me. Janet, I already paid for my hotel, bought the plane tickets, my wife had confidence in me—"

"Relax, DAG. Chill. I got 'em!"

I think I hear myself scream.

"Really? Oh . . . *my*! Thank you, thank you, thank you! I knew you'd come through. Like I said, I don't care where I'm sitting. Don't even care *if* I'm sitting."

"Oh, you're sitting all right. In fact, are you sitting down right now?"

"Yeah?"

"I got you the Platinum VIP Inaugural Package."

"The whatinum?"

"Top of the line. You got a car to take you to the event and bring you back to your hotel. You got two VIP seats. You're going to be sitting right near Barack. I'm talking *right* near him. Like next to him."

I'm gone. Sailing off into gaga land. In my mind I'm holding Barack Obama's arm, guiding him to the podium to recite the oath of office. The Secret Service drift back, out of my way, as I take the Bible from Michelle and hold it while Barack gets sworn in. In case he stumbles, I have memorized the oath and will cue him if he goes up on a line.

"DAG, did you hear what I said?"

"Huh? Ah, no, I was just, sorry—"

"I was saying that you are also going to the ball. The inaugural ball. The big one. VIPs only."

I don't speak for a solid thirty seconds. I feel a catch in my throat.

"I'm sorry, Janet. I'm just, you know . . . stunned. Now, let me ask you this, because I have to, and not that it matters, okay, it does matter a little, well, more than a little, in this economy . . . this is free, right? I don't have to pay anything for this Platinum VIP Inaugural Package?"

"Yep. It's free. We pulled it off." Janet lowers her voice, speaks as if she is a spy disclosing the launch codes. "DAG, people are paying over fifty thousand bucks for this package."

"Per ticket?"

"Per ticket."

"And I'm getting mine for free?"

"Totally. On the house. No charge."

"I don't know what to say. Janet, you are amazing."

"My pleasure. I will call you in the morning to give you further details."

I'm walking on air. I float around the house, find Christine, hug her, swing her around, do a little dance, and then shout, "Guess who's going to the inauguration?"

She whoops, we dance some more. Finally, breathless, we both lean against the kitchen counter.

"Tell me everything," Christine says.

"We have the Platinum VIP Inaugural Package. These tickets are going for fifty grand. But not for us. We have been comped, baby! Can you believe it?"

"Wow. *Wow.* What are the details?"

"Don't know the particulars yet. Janet is calling tomorrow with all the details."

Christine throws her arms around me. "I told you I had confidence in you."

A big hug.

Oh, yeah. This is all gonna work out fine.

✳   ✳   ✳

Janet doesn't call the next day with details. She doesn't call the day after that, either. Or the day after that.

I don't hear from her for a week.

I call her. She calls back. Leaves a message. We play phone tag for another week.

Finally we connect. Her voice sounds flat. Distant.

"David?"

"Hey, Janet, what's up?"

"Okay. Well."

I don't like the sound of this.

"There's been a problem."

"Problem? What kind of problem? What do you mean? What happened?"

"You have tickets to the inauguration."

"Great, great, great. So far I'm not hearing a problem. You had me worried there."

"They're just not the VIP platinum tickets."

Pause.

"Okay. What are they?"

"Yeah. See. What happened is."

Now she pauses. Catches her breath before she continues. Inhales, then puffs out tiny breaths as she speaks.

"There's been a last-minute rush. Nobody could have predicted this. So many people wanted those tickets that they actually stepped up and shelled out the money themselves. The money all goes to the Democratic Party. So I guess it's win-win in that sense. It's unbelievable. They just never anticipated this rush."

"So, what I'm hearing is that there are no VIP platinum inaugural tickets for me."

"No. Well, not for free."

"Not for free."

"Right. You could. If you wanted to." Janet clears her throat. "Pay."

"How much?"

"I can get you a discount. So it would be less than twenty-five grand."

"How much?"

"Ten."

"Ten thousand dollars? Each?"

"Yeah."

"Ten *thousand*?"

In that moment, during that phone call, I think about it. I consider it. I crunch some numbers. I move some money around in my head. I work through the math and consider . . . *consider* . . . spending $20,000 for two tickets. I think about the impact the election of Barack Obama has had on me. I think about how important this is both historically and personally. I try to do an instant visualization. I visualize myself at the inauguration and I visualize myself watching it here, in L.A., on TV. Then I visualize myself taking $20,000 out of the bank and—

I can't do it.

I go to Plan B. Spending $10,000 for one ticket. I'll go alone. Just me. Alone.

I definitely can't do that.

"What can I get for five thousand bucks?" I say.

Janet laughs.

I'm serious.

"Janet, I've already spent a small fortune on the hotel and airfare."

"I know. Let me call you back. There may be something else I can do."

I perk up. "You can get my VIP platinum tickets back?"

"No. Not gonna happen."

"Well, what then?"

"I'm gonna ask what you can get for five."

✳   ✳   ✳

Janet calls back in an hour.

"They can't get you anything for five."

You know what? I'm relieved. I feel as if I've been through the emotional wringer. Fuck it. We'll watch the inauguration on TV with friends. And I tried. I really did try.

"But, hey," Janet says brightly. "I got you tickets."

"You did?"

"Yes. You're in. But."

"But?"

"You've been downgraded."

"Uh-*huh*."

"No, David, listen. I got you really good tickets. They're not the platinum VIP tickets. They're not the twenty-five-thousand-dollar ones. But they are the next best thing. And they are free."

I'm perking up again.

"Which ones are these?"

A pause. A serious heavy-duty pause for effect.

"David, I got you—" And she practically whispers, "Purple tickets."

"Wow. Purple tickets. Should I be excited?"

"Very. Purple tickets are extremely important. Very much in demand. Go online. Go on eBay. Check it out. See how much people are selling these for. The purple tickets start at a couple thousand. That's where they start."

Now I am getting excited.

"Well, great. Okay. Purple tickets. Thank you, Janet. Thank you very much."

I do go online. I want to check out these purple tickets. Janet is right. Purple tickets are going for $2,000 and up. Then I go to a map of the inauguration and see that the purple ticket section is right next to the platinum VIP section. In fact, at certain spots, there is virtually no difference between the platinum VIP section and the purple section. Literally a fine line separates them. You'd have to be a fool to spend $10,000 or more for VIP platinum tickets when you can get the purple tickets right next to them for free. The color itself should give you a clue. Think about all the significant cultural references that contain the word *purple: The Color Purple,* the Purple

Gang, *Harold and the Purple Crayon, Purple Rain,* "Purple Haze," Deep Purple, "The Purple People Eater."

Fuck platinum. We're going purple!

I then get a little carried away. I go from freaking-out-that-I-don't-have-tickets-to-the-inauguration-I-have-been-shut-out to not-only-am-I-going-to-the-inauguration-but-I-have-the-special-purple-tickets.

I do this mainly with my family when I call them on the phone. I play it up.

"You hear that? David got tickets to the inauguration. He got the purple tickets. They're very special. Where you gonna be?"

"Close."

"He's gonna be *close.* Where you think he's gonna be with purple tickets? Yes. That's right. He got the purple tickets. Wait, hold on. Your brother's dying. He wants to know. Did you get the special purple tickets for *sure?*"

Yes, I play it up.

Which makes it even worse sitting here in the lobby of our hotel in Washington the day before the inauguration without any purple tickets. Having no idea where they could be. Or if they've been lost or stolen or if I ever had them at all. Or what I'm going to do.

Sitting in this lobby. In my own purple haze.

HIGH SCHOOL

1971.

Junior high school ends. Mercifully. No more worrying about getting my ass kicked. Or having to kick ass. On to high school. Now all I worry about is getting high and getting laid.

It's way easier to get high.

Even though I have a girlfriend.

Oh, we're physical. A lot. But in 1971, when you're fifteen, getting physical means that we mostly kiss. For hours. Like ten hours straight. Until I lose all feeling in my lips. I keep touching them to make sure that they didn't fall off. When I find them, they hurt to the touch. They're so sore I probably should put them in a sling.

Carla, my girlfriend, doesn't seem as affected by all our kissing. Or she won't admit it. When I see her around school, she asks, "How you doing?"

"Soh-ah. My mowff is soh-ah. Huts."

She laughs and shakes her head. "We gotta toughen you up."

I look at her with disbelief.

"Isn't your mowff soh-ah?"

"No." She laughs even harder, then winks and blows me a kiss. "See you tonight."

"Yeth," I say. "Gwate."

I wave and grimace from the pain pulsing through my mouth.

By sophomore year, I am still with Carla, but I have expanded my horizons. I am now also deeply interested in both music and drugs, which to me go together like spaghetti and meatballs, peaches and cream, pancakes and maple syrup.

In other words, you can't have one without the other.

You really can't listen to music without doing drugs. It wouldn't be right. Especially if you're going to a concert.

After much experimentation, discussion, and debate about which drug is the best for experiencing music live, my friends and I agree that the winner, hands down, is mescaline. Even better than the runner-up, pot. Mescaline takes you to a whole other level. Mescaline puts you into a zone.

Mescaline provides all the advantages of LSD with none of the hideous freak-out freaking out downsides. If you look into a mirror right after you drop LSD, you will see your face. But look in the mirror in an hour and you will see Peter Fonda. And not the Peter Fonda of 1971, who was a cool, hippie freak. The Peter Fonda of today, who's like eighty-seven. Mescaline gives you all the great hallucinations, colors, lights, kaleidoscopic effects, and superdazzling sound show without turning your brain into a hard-boiled egg. It's LSD lite. And you can take mescaline alone. You don't need a spotter. Another big advantage.

One night in the middle of the week, a Wednesday or Thursday, someone's older brother scores four tickets to see Black Sabbath downtown. I am so there. Next to the immortal Jimi—I would walk across miles of broken glass on my bare feet to see Hendrix live; I would eat broken glass; I would inhale broken glass—Black Sabbath is my number one.

Black Sabbath is a heavy metal band out of England featuring this young, whacked-out, wild nutcase lead singer named Ozzy Osbourne. The band has just released their brand-new album, *Paranoid,* and has hit the States on an American tour. One night only in Detroit. Tonight. We have to go. It's a must. A do-or-die. Of course, my friends and I are too young to drive, so we have to convince someone's mom to take us downtown, drop us off a safe distance from the concert, and pick us up at the same spot when the concert is over. Annoying. But necessary.

The arrangements for the night are admittedly complicated, but doable. They require precise planning and coordination. First, we check the time of the concert: 8:00 p.m. We get Phil Flaherty's mom—who lately seems to be willing to drive us whenever we want, anywhere, anytime, and pick us up anytime, anywhere—to be our wheel mom.

"Your mother is always driving us," I say to Phil. "Which is cool. I just have to ask one question. Why?"

"I don't know. My mother is a nice person."

"She's a very nice person," I say. "I'm a nice person, too. But I wouldn't drive our four sorry fucked-up asses five feet. Especially when we're high."

"She doesn't know we get high," Flaherty says.

"Please," I say, glaring at Flaherty to see if he really believes that.

"She doesn't," he says.

"Phil, *she* gets high," I say. "At least she did the night I was with her. *Oh!!!*"

Much laughing, giggling, slapping, and pinching. Very sophomoric because, well, we're *sophomores.*

Step two. Drugs. The easy part. Phil's cousin knows somebody who knows somebody, so we're set. Amazing. Procuring illegal substances of a hallucinogenic nature in the early '70s never seems like much of a hassle. Buy to get high. The stuff is everywhere.

Step three. Coordinating our highs.

The hard part.

Since the concert starts at 8:00, Phil's mother will pick us up at 7:45, which means we all have to drop the mescaline at exactly 7:30. The key is to time the high so we'll be peaking once Black Sabbath hits the stage and breaks into the first song. So important.

"We're all gonna drop at the same time," Phil informs us. "Otherwise someone is gonna be off on his own. Or peak too early. Or peak too late. Can't have none of that. So synchronize your watches, gentlemen."

We do. Then we stow our mescaline, prepare for a brilliant night.

"We should call each other," I suggest. "That way nobody fucks up."

We agree and design a phone tree. Phil will call me. We'll drop together, then I'll call Ray, while Phil calls Tony.

Perfect.

At 7:25, dressed all in black, I pace in my room, stereo on, Black Sabbath's "Iron Man" blasting. I mentally walk through each of the three steps. Wanna make sure everything's in place. Step one. The ride. Got it. Phil's mom. Our number-one wheel man. Check. Step two. Drugs. Got it. The mescaline's right here, shirt pocket. Glass of water. Nightstand. Check. Step three. Tickets. Shirt pocket, tight against the tickets. Check. Awesome seats, too. Third row! Close enough to catch some of Ozzy's spit.

The phone rings. Phil.

"Pill's on my tongue," he says.

I pop mine into my mouth.

"Mine, too," I say.

"And . . . drop."

Phil and I swallow at the same time. We gargle into the phone for verification. We hang up. I call Ray, Phil calls Tony. I dance over to my stereo, turn Black Sabbath *up*. Redline Ozzy. I air guitar the solo to "Iron Man," waiting for the mescaline to take effect. I'll know the m. has started when a six-foot checkerboard appears and starts dancing with me. Until then—

The door flies open. I jump three feet off the ground. My mother stands in the doorway.

"Mom. Damn. You should knock."

"I've been knocking for ten minutes, David," she says.

"Really? How come I didn't hear you?"

"It's the music—turn the music down."

"It's Black Sabbath. I'm getting revved up for the concert."

I resume my air guitar solo. My mother nods. Slowly. This I don't like. When my mother nods slowly, something's coming.

"I just got off the phone with your father," she says. "In this case we agree."

"On what?" I feel my voice crack.

"We don't want you to go."

"Where?" I say stupidly, knowing that I am fucked now in so many ways.

"You know where. The concert."

"Mom, please—"

"I'm not going to allow you to go, David. It's a school night. You're fifteen years old. You are not going. I'm sorry."

"Okay, see." I scratch my head. I blink. Once, twice. I stare at my mother and see a grid of blue, green, purple, pink, and yellow dots. "Mom, I don't think you understand. I need to go. I really . . . really . . . *need* to go."

And then the six-foot checkerboard appears and starts shimmying toward me. So funny. I giggle.

"David, are you all right?"

"Huh?"

"You're acting very strange. Do you have a temperature? Let me feel your forehead."

"Mom, please, this one time . . . just this one time . . . let me please . . . please . . . go to the Black Sabbath concert. I will come home right after, we will not stop . . . STOP! . . . anywhere. Please."

I drop to my knees, my hands folded. The giant checkerboard is smiling at me now.

"You know, David, I don't often change my mind."

I leap to my feet.

"Yes?"

"Seeing you tonight, I'm definitely not changing my mind."

She leaves, closes the door behind her. I silently mouth "No" as the giant checkerboard morphs now into a complex pattern of colors resembling a series of interconnecting octagons all with mouths, all singing the Black Sabbath trademark song, "Evil Woman."

Major . . . *major* . . . bummer . . . I am high as F-U-C-K!!

* * *

Of course, this night, this useless, fucked-up, concert-less night, I happen to drop the best mescaline in the history of mescaline. In the history of drugs. Period.

I'm flying. I plop on my bed and stare at the ceiling. Wow. Stunning. Miraculous stained-glass windows descend and flick by like a slide show. Can't count how many. Then plump happy checkerboard people bounce in and surround the bed. So soft. So puffy. I look into the overhead light and see a flickering, wavy lava lamp. Wowwwwww.

This all happens between 7:45 and 7:50.

What will I do to pass the next, oh, eight hours?

I call Carla.

She is doing homework. She has a paper due and a history quiz tomorrow.

"Hey, what's up, Carla?"

"Hey, David, what's up?"

"Nothin'. You know. This and that. Nothin'."

"I thought you were going to the Black Sabbath concert."

"Was."

"You're not?"

"No."

"What happened?"

"Moms said no. She said I can't go . . . because . . . it . . . is . . . a . . . SCHOOL . . . night."

This cracks me up. It may in fact be the funniest thing I've ever said or heard in my life. I laugh for at least five minutes straight.

"David, I have to write my paper. And I have to study for this test. I haven't even started—"

"Okay, okay, okay. Carla. Okay. Just one thing. And I will let you go. I promise. Just let me tell you this one, very important thing."

"And then you'll hang up so I can study?"

"Yes, yes. Absolutely."

"Okay. One thing."

"Here it is. Have you ever listened to *Electric Ladyland* by Jimi Hendrix? I mean really listened to it?"

"I don't think so. Not really. No."

"*No?* You have got to be kidding me. You have to listen to it. You have to. It's very important."

"David, are you high?"

"Whaaa—?"

"You are. I'm hanging up."

"Me? High? No. So, Carla. *Electric Ladyland.* It starts out with this amazing song, '. . . And the Gods Made Love.' The song is incredible."

"David, you said one thing."

"I know. *Electric Ladyland* by Jimi Hendrix. That's my one thing."

Carla sighs. In my mind's eye she cradles the phone against her shoulder and begins typing her paper. I keep talking. I go through every song on *Electric Ladyland,* all sixteen of them. I sing some of them, speak the lyrics, cry to a couple of them, laugh to the rest. I tell Carla she is a "Voodoo Chile" and that she has "Gypsy Eyes," and that we should "Come On (Let the Good Times Roll)."

She laughs.

Once at 9:45 p.m. and again at 1:32 a.m.

At 2:00 a.m., the mescaline takes me down and I get morose. I apologize. Yell about my parents. Cry for no reason at all. But I don't stop talking.

At 5:45 a.m. my mother wanders out of her bedroom and finds me sprawled on the kitchen floor. I pretend I'm asleep. She shakes her head, pours herself a glass of water, and goes back to bed. I continue my conversation with Carla, not realizing that she'd fallen asleep three hours earlier.

*   *   *

Sophomore year ends, and Carla and I take a break—I'm sad, but at least I get the feeling back in my lips. Junior year begins, and, pressured by my college counselor, who's just trying to do her job, and my parents, who are just doing theirs, being my parents, I start thinking about my future. I really don't want to. I kinda like hanging out, getting high, and just goofing around with my friends. I realize, sadly, that I can't do this for a living. I know I will be going to college. That's a given. But what will I go to college *for*? What will I study?

The fuck if I know.

I'm sixteen. I have no idea what I want to do with my life.

Well, that's not exactly true. I do know what I want to do. I actually have determined a very specific career path. Just not sure I want to tell the world. Yet. Until it happens. Because I think it might take a year or two for everything to fall into place.

See, I want to be a rock star.

For the time being, I believe this desire is best kept to myself.

When my mother asks me, "David, have you thought about what you want to do with your life? Do you know what field you might want to go into?" I shrug and mutter, "Idon'tknowma" because saying "Yes, I want to become a rock star, travel the world, trash my hotel room, get high, and have sex with hundreds of groupies" will lead to an uncomfortable discussion. Especially with my mother.

Here's the weird part.

I really think I have a chance to be a rock star.

I know I can sing. And lately, I've begun to write songs. I'm not confident that my tunes are ready to be played on the radio yet, but I'm working on that.

But the number-one reason I see myself as a rock star is that I love to perform. Now, not too many people know I love to perform because I will not sing or perform anywhere in public, meaning, at the moment, on the high school stage. No way I'm joining the high school drama club. I've checked it out. Too geeky and too gay. My plan is to become a rock star, not sing and dance on Broadway.

Besides, I don't need the drama club. I have a better place to perform. And that's what I do every Saturday night. Sing.

In my friend Phil's mom's car.

What a car. A flat gray Impala. There's something about the body shape and the design of the interior that gives Phil's mom's car perfect acoustics. The sound echoes off the upholstery, bangs in and out of the dash, circles around the front seat, floats into the back, and reverberates off the floor. The only other place that has acoustics this good is my shower. I think the inside of Phil's mom's Impala actually has my shower beat. It's like Phil Spector's Wall of Sound combined with Berry Gordy's Motown studio. If I could've stayed in that car, singing and performing, I definitely would've become a rock star.

So, Saturday nights we sing. But first, every Saturday afternoon, we arrange our Saturday nights with the same unwavering, intricate attention to detail and planning.

"Hey, Phil, what's up?"

"Hey, DAG, what's up?"

"Same old."

"What you wanna do tonight?"

"I dunno. What you wanna do?"

"I dunno. You wanna find a party?"

"Yeah, man, definitely. Let's find a party. I hear there's some happening parties tonight."

"You do? Cool."

"Hey, man, can you get your mom's car?"

"I don't know, man. I'll ask, but you know. It's touch and go. What if she has to go somewhere, man? Do something?"

"I hear you, man."

"Hey, DAG, any chance you can get your mom's car?"

"Naw."

Phil sighs. "I'll see what I can do."

Of course, Phil's mom never goes anywhere or does anything and is happy to give Phil the Impala every Saturday night. I wonder if she knows we use the car as a combination music studio and drug den. After our intricate Saturday night plan, we hit the streets, the four of us, friends since the seventh grade, share a joint or two, and look for parties, cruising in Phil's mom's Impala. Sometimes we find a decent party, which means we make a fifteen-minute cameo appearance, grab whatever food is available, stuff our faces and our pockets, leave, look for another party, cruise, and sing.

We always sing.

Sometimes we drive and sing. Mostly, though, we pull over to certain select spots and sing. What's strange is that these guys take the singing as seriously as I do. Because these Saturday nights, we don't just sing. We perform entire concerts.

Our opening number and best song, our signature, is Isaac Hayes's "Theme from *Shaft*."

What's great about "*Shaft*" is that each one of us is not only responsible for a specific vocal part but we're also responsible for creating the sounds of the instruments as well. I take the responsibility for the delicate *wah-wah-wah* reverb, a crucial component of the song. And if you fuck up with these guys, they will come at you.

"No, no, stop. You're not doing it right."

"What do you mean? That was right."

"It was not. It was fucked up. It's supposed to go *wah-wah-WAH*. You went *wah-WAH-wah*. It's fucked up, man. You're throwing the rest of us off. You're making '*Shaft*' sound like shit."

"Are you sure?"

Ron, big bass voice from the backseat. "We're sure. You fucking up the *wah-wah*s, man. We can't have that."

"We can't have it," Phil repeats, nodding, sucking on a reefer.

"Get it right," Ron says.

"Let me try it again."

"Hey, pass me that bag of chips, man."

"No food in the car, Ron. You know the rule. You have to take the chips outside."

"Chips aren't food. Chips are a snack. Give 'em here."

"Ron, chips are food," Tony says. "In my pocket I happen to have half a beef jerky. Now, a beef jerky is not food. It's food-*like*. It's satisfying and delicious, but it's not food. Same as Velveeta cheese."

"Just give me food or something that's food-*like*, I don't give a shit. I'm starving, man."

"Hey, Phil," Tony says. "How come we can't eat in your mom's car but it's okay to get higher than Jefferson Airplane?"

"All right," I say. "I think I got it."

We count down and hit the intro to "Theme from *Shaft*." I wail my *wah-wah-wah*s like I'm singing the last song on earth, and we are on it, all of us, all our "instruments" in synch, all our vocals crisp, clear, in perfect harmony. Then, without a word, we continue our concert with songs from Crosby, Stills, Nash & Young's live album, *Déjà vu*, ending with our rendition of their stirring antiwar song "Find the Cost of Freedom." I close my eyes, put a hand over my ear, and focus on my part. I do not want to disrupt the music or this moment. It's too important.

High school. Junior and senior years. I find my place. Find where I fit. Where I belong.

Sitting in Phil's mom's Impala, singing with my friends, in perfect harmony.

THE SECRET TO MARRIAGE

Barack Obama has been elected the first African-American president of the United States, but that's not enough for some people. No, they're not stopping there. These people say that Barack Obama has also achieved another high-ranking, *unelected* office. He is now, according to them, officially our first real-life magical Negro.

In case you don't know what this means, the magical Negro is a mythical figure, usually in movies, who just shows up one day—simply appears—to help out the white protagonist. Kinda like an angel. Think Clarence in *It's a Wonderful Life*. Only black. And not so whiny.

Actors such as Sidney Poitier, Morgan Freeman, Michael Clarke Duncan, and Will Smith have played the magical Negro, portraying characters like the brilliant and wise prisoner who happens to be shackled to Tim Robbins on the chain gang, or, in other movies, the clever caddy, the innocent and, sadly, executed prisoner, or the genius janitor. The magical Negro is a loner and never has any family, friends, or loved ones. He always comes across as unthreatening and supportive, wise but not a smart-ass, and black, but black like Barack Obama, not black like Al Sharpton or Snoop Dogg.

Frankly, I think white people talking about Barack Obama as the magical Negro have it wrong. Yes, he's articulate—as Joe Biden famously and insultingly called him; and Barack Obama still selected him to be his vice president—and he does seem genuinely wise, caring, and understanding. But if you focus on only these qualities, you make him seem less human and more like some myth, or comic book superhero, and not just the most qualified *man* to be president.

Plus, Barack Obama *is* the protagonist. He's not the sidekick. He's not the janitor sweeping the floor of the Oval Office late at night who gives advice to the president on everything from grooming tips to career guidance to life-changing wisdom. He is the fucking president.

The magical Negro would be the one sweeping up. He's got all the answers, but he's powerless. He would say to the president, "None of my business, but I wouldn't wear that blue suit to the press conference. And that tie? No. A fashion blunder. Lose it. It's an eyesore."

"Really, Rastus? Are you sure? What's wrong with my suit and tie?"

"Just don't look right. You mind lifting your legs? I gotta sweep away those dust bunnies, Prez."

The magical Negro's role is thankless. He's forced to spend the entire movie in some shit job, trying to get the hardheaded hero, some stiff, clueless white guy, to see the light.

"You really need to hug your son. And listen to your daughter when she talks about boy problems. Pretend you care. And be nicer to your wife. Maybe she'll stop drinking."

Of course, the classic example of the magical Negro is found in the movie *The Legend of Bagger Vance,* starring Will Smith and Matt Damon, and directed by Robert Redford.

First of all, Will is literally a *magic* "magical Negro" because he materializes out of nowhere to help the disillusioned Matt Damon.

"Where'd you come from, Bagger? How do you know so much about golf?"

We never know. Bagger gives vague answers. Matt doesn't press him. Fuck it. Bagger is a caddy and a mystic who dispenses great advice that at first sounds crazy.

"Try your putter instead of your sand wedge. That'll work better for you."

"Are you sure? Because, see, my ball is sitting in the *sand* trap. That's why I went for the *sand* wedge."

"Listen to me. Use your putter."

Long look at the magical Negro. Matt pulls out his putter. Holes it out.

"Amazing, Bagger. You're incredible. Why don't you play yourself? Why don't you compete?"

"Oh, no, I don't do that. I help others. I give advice. I don't actually do anything. That would conflict with my role—being a magical Negro put here in this caddy shack to help you, Matt Damon. So I'll just stay here, impart wisdom, and polish up your cleats."

I also think that the magical Negro is only magic in the white world. When he gets home, he's just a guy like any other guy.

"Hey, baby. I'm home from the golf tournament. Hard day giving advice to that thickheaded Matt Damon."

"You know what? I don't care how thickheaded he is, you're tracking mud through the house! Take your cleats off. Are you ignorant?"

"Don't talk to me like that, Wanda. I'm the magical Negro, remember?"

"I got some magic for your ass, motherfucker. Why don't you magically take out the trash? Magical Negro. Hey, Mr. Magical Negro, how about you magically add some zeroes to our checkbook and buy me a new motherfucking car, got-damnit. Magic, my ass. Right. You a magical Negro and I'm Oprah Winfrey."

It's possible that thanks to Barack Obama, along with the death of the angry black man, we just may be seeing the death of the magical Negro.

✳ ✳ ✳

Washington, D.C.

The day before the inauguration.

The truth is, I need some magic right now. I wouldn't mind a visit from Will Smith if he could help me out.

Because I'm still ticketless.

Somehow—I don't remember how and I don't remember when—Christine and I have relocated from the lobby of the hotel to our hotel room. It happens in a flash. Probably when I'm distracted on the phone for the third or fourth or fifth time, trying to connect with Janet, procurer of our purple tickets, leaving desperate voice-mail messages as I try to locate our special, coveted, and currently missing tickets to the inauguration. I do vaguely remember someone helping us with our luggage. Or maybe not. Maybe we got sucked into some time-travel vortex and, *whoosh*, got transported up to our room. If only I can do that with the inauguration. Close my eyes. Squeeze hard. Picture us sitting two rows in front of Barack Obama. And . . . *whoosh*. We're there.

That's Plan B.

Time travel. With a dose of visualization.

Plan A is to find a ticket scalper and pay like $100,000 for tickets that I already *have* but have not been delivered—hand-delivered, I was told—and placed into an envelope, a second envelope, next to the envelope that contains the keys to our room.

I'm really counting on Plan B.

Christine comes out of the bathroom, where she has neatly arranged her toiletries. She finds me where she left me ten minutes ago, sitting on the bed, immobile, frozen, too upset to move.

"This doesn't make sense," Christine says.

"What doesn't?"

"Janet seemed so sure that she got you the tickets."

"Yeah? Do you see an envelope with tickets?"

"It just doesn't make sense," Christine says again.

"Fuck sense," I say. "Here's the reality. We have no damn tickets. And I cannot get in touch with Janet. We are fucked!"

Christine sits at the far edge of the bed. If I shift my weight, she'll be on the floor.

"I'm just gonna have to bite the bullet," I say. "No other choice. I'm gonna have to call a ticket broker and pay like a billion dollars."

"That is ridiculous," Christine says.

"Do you have a better idea?"

"We have tickets!"

"Where?" I say, starting to lose it. "Where are the tickets? Show me where!"

Christine leaps off the bed and turns away from me. Suddenly, she seems to laser in on something on the nightstand. Between a chrome gooseneck lamp and the black digital alarm clock rests the envelope the hotel gave us—the envelope with the room keys. We haven't even opened it yet. The bellman opened the door for us.

"What's in here?" Christine says, picking up the envelope.

"The room keys," I say. "And a map, probably, shit like that. It's from the hotel."

"But you haven't opened it."

"No," I say. "Jillian at the front desk told me what she put in there."

"Maybe the tickets are in here," Christine says, turning the envelope over.

As my grandmother would say, I've got one nerve left and Christine's leaning on it.

"No, Christine, they're not. Janet said the tickets are in *another* envelope. An envelope that was supposed to be hand-delivered. This isn't the envelope. This is the envelope from the hotel with our room keys. THIS IS NOT THE ENVELOPE FROM JANET WITH THE PURPLE TICKETS!"

Rip.

Christine tears open the envelope. She spreads the envelope wide, peers inside. She pulls out two key cards, a colorful map of the city, and two cards for complimentary breakfast. And then she dips two fingers inside and plucks out two event-type tickets with purple borders.

Extremely purple.

She turns them over in her hands, examining them as if they are rare and mysterious treasures, artifacts she has never seen the likes of before.

"What are *these*?" she says, pretending to be confused. "Are these—? No. They can't be. But, wait, they are tickets. And they are purple. And they do have 'The Inauguration of President Barack Obama' written on them. No. These can't be the tickets."

"Okay," I say. I feel about as dumb as I have ever felt in my life. "I, okay. May I . . . see them?"

Christine slaps the tickets onto the nightstand. She lies noisily on the bed, props herself against the headboard, making a huge production in which she uses all the pillows, including any that previously might have been mine. She kicks off her shoes. Crosses her ankles. Gets comfortable. Settles in.

"Aha," I say, like I'm the lead redheaded dude on *CSI: Miami.* "See, what she did—it's obvious now—is she put the tickets in the same envelope, as the, you know, keys and stuff."

"Is that what she did?" Christine says, eyes widening in horror.

"Yeah," I said. "That's what she did. I should probably call Janet. I left her a panic message or two."

"Four," Christine says. "You left her four out-of-your-head panic messages."

I duck my head, try my most charming smile. Christine shakes her head and reaches for the remote. Can't read her. She's either very cool, laughing on the inside, icing me a little, just trying to make me sweat. Or inside she's seething and is going to give me the cold shoulder for several hours. Either way, I'm fucked.

"We're all pretty tense," I say. "It's a tense time."

"I'm not tense," Christine says. "Are you?"

"Me? No. Not at all. Maybe a little. A tad."

"You need to calm down," Christine says. "Take a hot bath. Or a cold shower. Have a drink. Get a massage. Something."

"I do," I say. "You're right. I can get carried away. Not often. On occasion. Once in a rare while."

Christine rolls her eyes and begins to channel surf.

I look at her and decide to take a wild swing at the ball. What the hell. I've messed things up so far. Made a fool out of myself. Got nothing to lose. Might as well go for the fences.

"You wouldn't, by any chance, want to call Janet—"

I duck a flying pillow.

Which is so cool because somebody else might have thrown the remote. Or come after me with that gooseneck lamp. Not Christine. She has her shit way together. I am very happy about this. Because even when I am—rarely—difficult or an asshole, or pigheaded, she puts up with me.

So here, then, is the secret to marriage in two words:

Marry up.

I did.

11

PURPLE CRUSH

Walking through Georgetown the night before the inauguration, Christine and I feel it everywhere, all around us, engulfing us.

Constant, continuous, unmistakable.

The feeling of JOY.

It is as pervasive and powerful as a scent, a sweet aroma that overtakes you and dominates the air, virtually becoming the air itself. We breathe it in. We walk and inhale massive gulps of nothing but total celebration. As we pass people on the street and others coming in and out of stores and restaurants, we feel the joy seeping out of everyone else's pores as well. You can't shake it. I don't want to.

Hell, I wish I could bottle it. Bring it home. Spread it around. Toss it into our air, into everyone's air, drop it from above into our atmosphere.

We know where it's coming from. It comes from the feeling that has been born not just from the thought that real change lies ahead but also from sheer, unadulterated anticipation. We are so anxious. So happily anxious. I just never thought it would feel this strong, this . . . *wonderful.*

And so Christine and I walk in silence, holding hands, holding on, sucking down the joy as if it is oxygen, never, ever, wanting this feeling to stop.

✻　✻　✻

Although Barack Obama will not be sworn in as our forty-fourth president until noon, I plan to arrive at our gate, the Purple Gate, by 9:00 a.m. On this, Christine and I agree. Well, to be fair, she thinks we should get there by 8:00 a.m. I say to myself as I take my sweet time getting ready—

Have you lost your mind?

Four hours before the inauguration?

Standing around doing nothing, on our feet, in the frigid cold for four hours?

Three hours before will give us plenty of time.

We step outside our hotel. Everyone I know has warned me to be prepared to walk to the National Mall, since there won't be a cab available anywhere in the city. We walk three feet, I see a cab turn a corner, I stick up my hand, and—*vroosh*—the cab skids to a stop in front of us. I tell the cabdriver to take us to the Purple Gate. He shakes his head knowingly, then zooms in that direction.

Takes us less than seven minutes. Not another car in sight.

At 9:00 a.m., when we arrive at the Purple Gate—actually, when we *attempt* to arrive at the Purple Gate—we get out of the cab and walk into what appears to be easily a million people, give or take a hundred thousand. I won't look at Christine. Don't have to. I can feel the stink eye boring into my brain like an electric drill.

In fact, the crowd builds slowly, kind of sneaks up on you. At first it doesn't seem like anything too bad. We start walking, about a half mile away from the gate. We have no indication of what lies ahead. We speed by a few slow walkers, curl in and around a couple of clusters of folks in ski parkas and long coats with Obama buttons and hats, then slither through a line of people blocking our way, then, *bam*. Stopped. A mass of humanity fills the rest of the way from here on, spreading across the sidewalk and street, well short of the Purple Gate, which we can barely make out in the distance.

We are a parking lot of people. Slammed shoulder to shoulder. Surrounded on all sides. Body to body. Locked in tight. Nobody is moving. Can't. Each of us has staked out a couple of inches of breathing room and that's it. That's all we can get. That's all we're allowed.

I extend myself to my full height to get a better view. I see a wave of people stretched from my spot to the Purple Gate in the distance, a hundred yards away. A dozen cops stand in front of the gate, a shaky blue line of defense between the million of us and the now slightly swaying Purple Gate. I don't like the cops' odds. But the vibe here is anything but nervous or aggressive. I feel only the calm, cool Barack Obama vibe that has been spreading over us for days.

The sudden *a-ooga* screech of a siren jolts me. The gut-rattling screech is followed by a second, even harsher, siren wail. The sound mixed with the frigid morning air hits me like a cold stab in the ear.

"Please move aside!"

A mechanical voice crackling through a megaphone. A tremor of shuffling. A quiver of movement. Generic weight shifting side to side. But nothing that's real. No one's giving up their spot. Not based on some disconnected metallic voice.

"Ambulance! Ambulance coming through!"

Now people murmur. I'm jostled, bumped back into a stranger, tossed against Christine. Instinctively, we clamp closer into each other, creeping, creeping, creating a tiny path, maybe large enough for a tricycle, and then recoil from a third siren burst.

Murmuring morphs to grumbling. I start to shout, "We're trying here! We're trying to let you by!" but someone nearby beats me to it.

"We've got to get this ambulance in!"

A metallic, mechanical plea.

Defying physics and geometry, we scrunch even tighter together and separate into two halves and clear a path, a miracle like the parting of the Red Sea. An ambulance appears behind us and then next to us, jerking and inching ahead, as if there is a first-time driver at the wheel. Christine clings to me. I'm practically wearing her.

"Ow!"

"What?" I say, trying to turn to her, not able to, my neck and shoulders clamped tight by my wife on one side and what appears to be a family of dairy farmers from Wisconsin on the other.

"The ambulance guy! He almost ran me over!"

"Relax. He can't run you over. He's going two miles an hour."

"He brushed me. I felt it."

"All right," I say. "I think you're okay. It's just a little crazy here."

"It's insane."

The ambulance creeps forward, its boxy rear just ahead of us now. The crowd floods back in, the crush resumed.

"When we get to the gate, it's going to be nuts," Christine says. "We may get separated."

"It's possible," I admit.

"I should hold my own ticket just in case."

I nod. I pull a glove off with my teeth, fish my hand into my pocket, and pull out one of the purple tickets. Christine snatches it, stuffs it into her coat pocket.

"I think we'll be all right," I say, standing on my toes. The ambulance inches closer to the Purple Gate. The line of police splits, clears a path. "We just have to stay really close. Stick tight."

As the ambulance heads into the mall area, picking up speed from two miles per hour to ten, the crowd surges. I'm shoved five feet forward, plowed into by a wrecking ball of bodies behind me, then the crowd closes up, sealing me in as before.

"You were right," I say to my wife. "We should've gotten here earlier."

I turn and give her my warmest and most conciliatory smile.

But she's gone.

I've lost her.

✳　✳　✳

Oh, well.

I'm sure she'll turn up. No reason to freak out about it. Because as I look at the horde of people crushed up against me and around me, people who are practically on top of me, literally thousands of people, I realize that you will lose the person next to you, now or eventually, unless you are chained together at the wrist. I feel like a very optimistic Katrina survivor. Maybe I need to climb on the roof of a car, make a sign out of cardboard, and write in shoe polish "Send Help . . . Hope and Change!"

Best thing to do is chill. Enjoy the moment. Experience history. We will compare notes, break down the game tape, later, back at the hotel.

Someone wonders about the time. A flock of cell phones chirp.

"Nine fifteen," a voice calls.

"Almost three hours to go," someone else says.

"I'm eighty-one years old," a thin, shaky voice seeps out. "I could use a chair."

A roar of laughter.

Then a deep baritone sings out from somewhere, expressing the sentiment we all feel despite the crush of humanity and the frigid temperatures, articulating the emotion that prevails in that space, at that time, literally waiting for the hope to begin.

"Don't worry. We won't let you fall."

12

HATED IT!

Strange how you bond when you're smacked up tight against a million strangers. You feel oddly close. The comfort of strangers, I guess. We talk, we laugh, we share anecdotes.

It's amazing how in a crowd of one million you can close your eyes, drift away, and end up feeling . . . alone.

Three hours of waiting for your life to change.

While, at the same time, my life passes in front of my eyes, as if this is my last moment on earth. *Whoosh*. My life passes not in stories but in snapshots. It feels as if it all happened so fast. Five minutes ago, I am in high school, about to begin college.

I remember the nights I spent in Phil's mom's Impala, singing "Theme from *Shaft*" followed by those lovely, melodic protest songs of Crosby, Stills, Nash & Young. Beautiful nights. Nights of harmony. Yeah, we got high, and slammed each other hard, but those were nights of innocence. And laughter. And like this day, filled with joy. I wonder where Phil is and who he has become and whether the presidency of Barack Obama means as much to him as it does to me.

So many ends and beginnings.

I graduate high school and enroll at the University of Michigan. The school is massive and I struggle to fit in. I don't know much about myself. I know I have this ache. It's odd. Hard to admit. It's an ache to perform. I ache to sing my songs and entertain. But I don't want to disappoint my parents, who, based on my good high school grades, see me becoming a doctor or a lawyer. I hear my father's voice echoing in my head, "You have to work for yourself, David. That's the only way a black man can ever have any control over his life."

I agree with my father. I take his words to heart. I have just two issues. Being around sick people makes me feel faint, so I can't be a doctor. And I hate the sight of blood, so I can't be a lawyer.

Following my heart, I drift over to the theater department. I'm weirdly attracted to the road companies who come in and perform plays at the Power Center for the Performing Arts. There is something about these traveling professional artists, these performers. They dress differently, act cooler, and seem more confident. They have created a tight kind of family. There is something exotic and romantic about them. I don't get too close. I observe, from a distance, track their comings and goings, as if I am an archaeologist on a dig. I'm mesmerized by them. I try to imagine myself one of them. It seems impossible, unrealistic, about as likely as my running away and joining the circus.

While I'm infatuated by these road company performers, I'm in love with the idea of creating and performing my own music. I've become totally taken in by the new punk music scene that's happening in New York. I read the *Village Voice* and *Creem* magazine religiously, devouring the work of Lester Bangs, Lisa Robinson, and Robert Christgau, who report on such exciting new bands as the Clash, the Sex Pistols, Iggy Pop and the Stooges, the Ramones, and Television, all of whom play at new clubs in New York, such as CBGBs.

And what am I doing?

Sitting in Sociology 101 in a sterile lecture hall in the middle of three hundred faceless freshmen, or wandering aimlessly through the Quad, or sitting slumped over a pitcher of beer that I haven't really touched at the Pretzel Bell, with people I don't really know.

I feel as if my life is passing me by.

I remember several nights sitting at the dining room table with my mother. I'm fifteen. I'm listening to Hendrix, of course, whose version of "All Along the Watchtower," besides shaking me up, has introduced me to the music and lyrics of Bob Dylan. I buy a book of Dylan lyrics, devour them, study them. The book becomes my bible. One night at the dining room table I share Dylan's songs with my mother.

We sit together, going over the book, song by song, line by line. I read the lyrics to her softly. I see surprise in her eyes.

"This is what I listen to, Mom," I say. "Do you understand why?"

She nods. "I think so," she says. "It's poetry." She flips to another Dylan song. "Read this one to me."

I do. When I finish, I look up at her. There are tears in her eyes.

"I understand this, David," she says. "I understand."

Which means, unlike so many parents I know, she understands me. She's not judging. Not criticizing. Just understanding.

By the end of freshman year, I decide that I can't stay in college anymore. It takes months of feeling lost, bored, and confused, and finally realizing, shockingly, that I'm surrounded by some of the dumbest people I've ever met. I need to get out. I need to go to New York. I can't allow the punk movement to continue without me. I have enough money saved to move and get started, barely. But I know that the hardest part will be telling my mom. Every time I imagine her reaction, envision the look on her face, I back down, almost talk myself out of leaving. I do know that I can't tell her face-to-face.

The night I leave I call her from the airport at eleven o'clock. She breaks down, sobs, begs me to come home just for the night. If I do that, I know I will never go. I promise to call her the moment I land. Starting to choke up, I hang up before I lose it, too.

I arrive in New York with a few hundred dollars and a backpack full of songs. I spend the first night at the Chelsea Hotel, which is a little less glamorous than its reputation, then move into the Chelsea YMCA, a well-known gay hangout, well known apparently to everyone in New York City but me. After a week of sleeping in my clothes, feeling way too nervous and uncomfortable, I find an apartment on the Lower East Side, between Avenues A and B. Actually, "apartment" may be too upscale. "Closet" is more like it. Unfurnished, fifth-floor walk-up, with a stunning, unobstructed view of a Dumpster, featuring a ceiling that leaks like a shower, but only when it rains—and all these amenities for only $115 a month, plus utilities. Furnishing my home is fun and reasonable. I find an old mattress on the street, haul it up the five flights, and lay it across a base of empty milk cartons. Voilà. Furnished! Set up now in my New York showplace, I make the rounds of coffeehouses and alley clubs, audition my songs, and—surprise!—get hired to perform a couple of nights a week! I've made it! I'm an overnight sensation.

Well, my paycheck and tips don't come close to covering my rent, so I'm forced to find another job. I land a fabulous part-time gig just around the corner from my apartment, every kid's dream job—working at an ice cream store.

It's a trip living in New York. I'm singing, performing, hearing live music, and, mostly, scooping out ice cream. It only takes a couple of months for the glamour to wear off. Soon, my work at the ice cream store intensifies. One guy quits and another guy rarely shows up. I'm asked to pick up the slack. I could use the money. I cover for both guys, pulling fifteen-hour shifts, which—except for my contracting carpal tunnel syndrome in my ice cream scooping wrist—doesn't bother me, because my coffeehouse gigs are starting to dry up, and the ones that don't, pay a pittance. At the moment, Marshall Crenshaw has the market cornered on catchy pop songs, and even though I love punk, I'm not sure the music world is ready for a black Johnny Rotten.

Then one night at the ice cream store, my life changes.

Around midnight. I am nearing the end of my third straight fifteen-hour shift. I am way beyond exhausted; I have left "exhausted" in the dust. I am well into the land of loopy, which is just north of buzzed and wacko.

Guy walks in. Beat-up leather jacket. Lotta hair. Confident air. Genuine smile.

He orders an ice cream cone.

"One scoop or two?"

"Two."

"Sugar cone or waffle."

"Well, hmm—"

I start tapping my feet.

"Take your time deciding," I say. "We don't close for an hour."

Then, ridiculously, because I am so buzzed from exhaustion, I make up a tune, using his order for my lyrics—

"One scoop or two, sugar cone or waffle, make the right choice, 'cuz one of them is awful."

I move into a dance, a little soft shoe, a little disco, then, still singing this song, using the scooper as a microphone, I jump onto the counter. I sing, I dance, and the whole time this guy, this customer in the beat-up leather jacket, is gaping at me. Can't tell if he's mesmerized or horrified. But I know he can't take his eyes off me.

I finish with a flourish, drop to one knee.

The guy applauds.

I bow and hop off the counter.

"Thank you very much," I say, milking him for my applause. "No, please. Thank you. And since you had to endure this moment of insanity, your ice cream cone is on the house."

"That was unbelievable," the guy says.

He's dead serious. I peer into his eyes to see if he's high. Nope.

"Well, you know, I've been working fifteen hours straight, I'm a little batty."

"That's not what you are. Do you want to know what you are?"

I'm not sure where this is going, so I just shrug.

"You are an actor."

I stop in midscoop.

"What?"

"You are an actor," the guy in the leather jacket repeats. "My name is Greg."

"Hey, Greg, what's up? I'm DAG."

"You're wasting your life here, man," Greg says. "I'm serious. I'm an actor, too. Listen, here's my number." He grabs a pen on the counter and scribbles his information on a napkin. "I want you to call me. You definitely got chops, but you need training. Classes. You have to learn technique. I'll bring you over to my acting school. I can get you in. Then I'll introduce you to my agent. You have to do this. Acting is your life's calling."

Maybe because I'm so loopy, or maybe it's because it's so late, or maybe I'm dreaming, or maybe I stand there for a crazy long time, but when I turn back around, I'm holding a double-scoop ice cream cone in my hand and Greg is gone, disappeared. It's as if he was a mirage.

"I'm an actor," I say to myself. "Whatever."

But in the deepest part of me, I know that this is the truth.

✳   ✳   ✳

I call up a friend and tell him all about Greg.

"You may be an actor, DAG, I dunno," my friend says. "But I'll tell you what this dude Greg is. Gay."

"Really? You think so?"

"You are so clueless, man. It's obvious. Have you seen *Midnight Cowboy*?"

"Well, yeah, but it's not like that. Although, come to think of it, he did wear a leather jacket like Jon Voight. No cowboy hat, though."

"He wants you to suck his dick, man. Can't you see that?"

"Get outta here. He wants to help me out."

"Yeah. He wants to help you out unzipping his pants, dude."

I have to admit that the idea of Greg's being gay never crossed my mind. Granted, I am only nineteen, new to New York, and a little naive. I wouldn't call myself a street kid. Remember, my idea of a big Saturday night was sharing a joint with three other guys and singing "Theme from *Shaft*." With harmony. And I was the wah-wah pedal. I suppose it's possible that Greg is gay. But I'm not. The only thing he's getting off me is free ice cream.

By the way, I don't have a problem with gay people. Didn't then. Don't now. I'm totally fine with gay people getting married. In fact, I want gay men to experience what I experience. Gay people, I want you one day to wake up next to the person you once thought was perfect and then, whew . . . face unshaved for three days, breath stinking, breathing on you with that dog breath, farting in bed, his body making noises you've never heard in a human, and all you can think is, *How can I kill this person?*

Welcome to my nightmare. So, yes, please, gay people, get married.

I want to see that married look in gay people's eyes. The look you see on guys standing with their wives at Home Depot, or the super-market, or the mall. That "get me the hell out of here" look. It's only fair.

I want to go up to some gay married guy at Home Depot and say, "Hey, what's up, man?" and get back that look.

I will remind him, "You wanted to get married. You wanted to be accepted by society just like the rest of us. You happy now? I tried to warn you."

Greg is not gay. A few days later he comes back into the ice cream store with his girlfriend. They're wearing matching leather jackets and are all over each other. She, too, is an actor. Greg tells me about his career. He acts in Off-Broadway plays and recently landed a re-curring role in a soap opera. He studies at The Neighborhood Play-house, a well-known, highly respected acting school that trained the likes of Gregory Peck, Steve McQueen, and Robert Duvall. He invites me to sit in on a class.

For the next few weeks, I hang with him and his girlfriend. I audit several classes at The Playhouse, meet his agent, work on a couple of scenes with Greg. It takes me about ten minutes to get bit-ten by the acting bug. Once I'm bitten, I'm done. Hooked for life. Weird how quickly it happens. Before I met Greg I hadn't thought of myself as an actor at all. Now I can't see myself as anything else.

At Greg's urging, I apply to The Neighborhood Playhouse. I meet with the founder, the legendary Sanford Meisner, who, after an hour-long interview, accepts me into the program without an audition. Being an actor makes so much more sense than becoming a rock star. I can act forever. I can get old as an actor. I can do *On Golden Pond* and perform Shakespeare into my seventies. I don't see myself wearing leather pants with my shirt off playing rock music into my seventies, unless I'm playing nursing homes and condo clubhouses. Think I'll go with acting.

One minor technicality.

Money.

As in, I don't have any.

I can stay in New York, attend The Neighborhood Playhouse, but that means I'll have to work at least one more job to afford my tuition and the closet I call my apartment.

Or I could go back to college. Which my parents will pay for.

Guess what I did.

Multiple-choice quiz time. I decide to:

(A) Stay in New York, study acting, and work three shit jobs.

(B) Go back to college, study acting, and have my parents pay.

If you chose (A), you were dropped on your head as a child.

*   *   *

Snapshots from then to now.

I go back to the University of Michigan. To make my parents happy, I major in radio, television, and film, and minor in journalism. They believe that this is less frivolous than acting and will give me something to fall back on. I guess they believe I could fall back and become a teacher or a television repairman. Truth is, all I do is act. I act in everything from serious drama to musicals. Early on, I'm cast in *Othello,* but not as the Moor. This is cool because it allows me to walk around campus saying, "Yeah, I just got cast in *Othello.*"

If anyone asks, "Wow, you're Othello?" I just say, "Uh-huh, close."

I graduate University of Michigan and attend grad school at Yale, where I'm in a class with a bunch of powerful actors, including the legendary Charles Dutton. I complete my MFA, acting for pretty much two straight years. I move to New York, land the title role in *The First,* a musical based on the life of Jackie Robinson, get cast in films such as *Streamers* and *A Soldier's Story,* receive nice acclaim, a Tony nomination, and I'm off and running.

And then my second life-changing moment arrives.

* * *

1989. I have just wrapped *I'm Gonna Git You Sucka,* Keenen Ivory Wayans's comic spoof. The movie is a hit and Keenen is red hot. He parlays his success into a TV deal with Fox to write and produce what he describes as an all-black *Saturday Night Live.* He asks me to audition.

I'm not sure.

Even though I had a blast doing *Sucka,* and I know I can be funny, and I was voted class clown in elementary, middle, *and* high school, I still see myself as a serious actor. I don't have a stand-up act, I don't have material, I don't have a bunch of characters I do. Keenen insists. He can be persuasive. Plus it's pilot season. That year I've tried out for more than thirty sitcoms and pilots and have been cast in exactly none. I really don't have much to lose.

I fly to Los Angeles from my home in New York and audition along with two up-and-coming comedians—Chris Rock and Martin Lawrence. I think they're hilarious.

They don't get cast.

I do.

Except I'm not sure I want to do the show.

"It'll be fun," Keenen says. "You'll be working with all your friends. Come on."

He makes a solid point. But I'm both a serious actor and, frankly, scared about doing a weekly hour-long comedy-sketch show.

So I turn it down.

I move back to New York to resume my serious acting career, having turned down a network television show so I can make a dollar fifty a week playing multiple roles in repertory at the Great Lakes Shakespeare Festival.

The day after I return to New York, Kim Wayans, Keenen's sister, calls. She is blunt.

"You just made the biggest mistake of your life," she says. "Now get back here and do this show."

The only thing she doesn't say is "Or else." Man. The way she talks, I'm scared now *not* to do it.

So I change my mind. I move back to Los Angeles, and for the next five years—the greatest and most insane five years of my show business life—alongside true comic geniuses Keenen, Damon, Jamie Foxx, and Jim Carrey, I appear every week in the cast of *In Living Color.*

* * *

Jim Carrey calls the show "historic." A TV critic calls it "hip-hop television." A music critic calls it groundbreaking because we showcase for the first time musical acts such as Digable Planets, the Wu-Tang Clan, and Public Enemy.

Me, I'm just trying to get laughs.

Since I don't come to the show armed with a repertoire of funny characters I can draw from, I have to start from scratch. One of my favorite characters is created by Larry and Marc Wilmore. Hanging out in their office, I listen to their hilarious stories about the barbershop they went to as kids. It was owned and run by this mean old black guy named Lewis. He was angry all the time, screaming his opinions about every subject under the sun while paying no attention to what he was doing with his customers' hair. Scared the hell out of them. I laughed because I had a similar experience. All black comics I know had a favorite barbershop and a barber they feared who always messed up their haircut.

In the barbershop, there was a chart of different afro hairstyles on the wall, facing the barber chairs, that we later re-created for the show. This chart was Lewis's Bible. To top it off, Lewis had a short fuse. As in, *everything* pissed him off. Including his customers.

"Who's next? You? Little man. Hurry up. Move your ass. I don't got all day. Sit in the chair, fool. Now what haircut you want?"

"Well, you know, I was thinking this time—"

"Point to the wall, motherfucker."

"I want it faded on the—"

"Point to the motherfucking *wall.* Can't you see the motherfucking *chart? Point to the motherfucking chart.*"

"Oh. Okay. I want the number three."

"Well, got-damnit, why the fuck didn't you say so? *Globetrotter* coming up!"

So Jamie Foxx and I play two inept barbers who pontificate about every possible subject while completely destroying our customers' hair. I love these characters. Whenever I play that old barber, I feel like I'm in the pocket: I know that old guy inside out. And I love working with Jamie. We riff off of each other for days. One time, incredibly, we get a chance to cut James Brown's hair.

For the record, James Brown is one of my all-time music heroes. To me, he is an R & B god. And now he's coming on the show to do a guest spot and the producers put him in our barbershop sketch! One condition. While the whole sketch is about how we mess up his hair, we are given strict instructions "Not to touch a follicle of Mr. Brown's hair." The hair department has pinned a small piece of fake James Brown hair to the back of the real James Brown's head. His wife slash manager slash hair stylist hovers close by repeating the mantra, "Do not, under any circumstances, touch Mr. Brown's hair." The producers roll cameras and Jamie and I start the scene. In walks the legendary James Brown (hold for applause). He sits in the barber's chair, and we are off and running. We get about six inches away from the fake hair we are supposed to cut and James Brown hops out of the chair, yells his one line, and runs out of the set. Stunned, Jamie and I stand there looking at each other, desperately trying not to crack up.

Then Damon and I play two gay film critics, Blaine Edwards and Antoine Marryweather, in what will become one of the show's most popular segments, "Men on Film." We start each segment by saying together, "Welcome to Men on Film."

Damon, as Blaine, follows by saying, "Where we look at movies—"

As Antoine I add, "From a male point of view."

We review real, straight, movies, pointing out scenes, dialogue, and action that in our outrageous view would appeal to gay culture. When we don't like something in a film, we scream together, "Hated it!" followed by two finger snaps and a circle or whatever hand gesture we decide to do that week. "Hated it!" becomes one of the signatures of the show.

Most black people I talk to or hear about love *In Living Color.*

Not all.

During one episode we do a bit called "Black *Jeopardy!*" with celebrity contestant Mike Tyson, played by Keenen. One of the *Jeopardy!* answers that the host, played by Jim Carrey, reads is "Fee Fi Fee Fi Fee Fi Fo." Keenen as Mike Tyson excitedly slams his buzzer and responds with the correct question: "What's my phone number?"

Hilarious, right?

It was to me. Not so much to Mike Tyson.

A couple of weeks later (Keenen tells me) Mike Tyson, then the most feared human being alive, rolls up on him in a club. He has seen the show and wants to have a conversation. Mike comes up on him so fast that Keenen can't duck him. Keenen tries to convince himself that Mike is an intelligent man who knows we were just playing. Probably coming over to congratulate him and tell him to keep up the good work.

He and Mike shake hands. Then Mike brings up the *Jeopardy!* sketch.

"That was so funny," Mike says in his high-pitched voice. He suddenly whirls on Keenen and grabs him in a hug. Not the kind of hug you give your brother or best friend or wife. More like a bear hug you give someone when you're trying to knock the wind out of him, forever. Not wanting to show fear, Keenen holds his ground.

"You like to make fun of people, don't you?" Mike whispers in Keenen's ear.

"Well, see—"

He doesn't finish his sentence because Mike bites his neck.

Doesn't break the skin. But bites him hard enough to leave a mark. Like the mark of Zorro.

"Yeah," Mike says. "You like to tell those jokes, don't you?"

Keenen laughs, but inside a voice is screaming, *Holy shit!* Then as quickly as he strikes, Mike releases Keenen and moves off. Everyone breathes a sigh of relief.

✳ ✳ ✳ **13** ✳ ✳ ✳

THE MOMENT

We're moving toward the Purple Gate!

At least I think we are. It's subtle. Almost imperceptible. But unmistakable. A tiny tug at my back. I push forward at least an inch. Maybe two.

There it is again. Oh, yeah! We are surging now. Pushing forward at least two inches this time. The cattlelike crowd, the million or more of us, shove ahead like a monstrous human wedge, grabbing another two inches, plowing toward the banner ahead that reads "Purple Gate" flapping above us, only a few hundred feet in the distance.

Another little push and I am now at least an entire foot from my last spot. The way we're surging, I have every confidence we will be inside the National Mall in less than an hour and I will be able to take my place in the exclusive purple section, a mere arm's length away from President-elect Barack Obama and his family. Spittin' distance.

I wonder if he watches the *Chocolate News*. I bet he does. He seems to have his pulse on popular culture. And while it's obvious that he's smarter than the last guy—well, I mean, seriously, who isn't?—Barack Obama seems to get an unbelievable amount of stuff accomplished in the course of a day. It's almost as if he's been allotted more than twenty-four hours. It's like God said to him, "You are going to be president of the United States. I'm gonna take care of that. But since you will be the first African-American president and there will be a lot of pressure on you, you're gonna need a little extra something to help you out. Here's what I'm thinking. I'm gonna give you more hours in the day than everyone else. Instead of twenty-four hours, I'm giving you thirty-six. This is so you can have some time to chill, get some sleep, watch the NCAA Tournament, enjoy some quality time with Michelle, play with your daughters—in addition to having to clean up the chin-high pile of crap the previous administration left you. Just don't tell anybody, because I'm not really supposed to do shit like that."

We take another step. And another. A slow and steady push forward, feeling like a pulse through the crowd. For the first time in an hour, this feels like real progress. I wonder if I can see my wife. I twist my head left, then right, and shout into the mass, "Christine!"

"Here!" three people shout back.

None of them is my wife.

Ahead, I hear a roar. It trickles back, a sound wave bouncing over and through us. Miraculously, the jam of people in front of me shoves forward, vacating their spots, covering the distance between our position and the Purple Gate in less than thirty seconds. I jog behind them, pressing my palm in front of me, which lands on the back of a shiny black ski parka. The swaying banner announcing the Purple Gate hangs above me. I'm ten feet away—five rows of people—from the gate itself and about to enter the Mall's grounds.

Then, *wham,* we stop. Almost like we hit a cartoon skid. A collective moan of disappointment and frustration rings out. I'm one of the major moaners. I'm not really feeling angry. That's not what it is. There is no anger today. Today is about experiencing something that surpasses anger no matter what.

But right now I need to find my center. I need to remain cool and calm, the way Barack Obama always seems to. The man was born with a supremely powerful chill factor. After enduring years of being overheated, nationally, we need to incorporate some of that chill.

Breathe. That's how we start. Start with a breath. Remember how to breathe—

I conjure up those moments in my life that have required controlled, deep breathing, the kind of slow, cleansing breaths that prevented me from screaming, going berserk, and being tempted to kick through the closest wall—

Going onstage on Broadway for the first time.

Falling in love.

The birth of my daughter.

Breathe. In. Out.

"I'm calm, I'm very, very calm," I say as quietly as I can. "I'm going to get inside the National Mall and sit down in my excellent seats because I have purple tickets."

"I have purple tickets, too," someone in front of me says.

"So do I," another voice calls back.

"Me, too," a voice behind me says.

"We all got purple tickets," a deep Barry White–like voice sings out.

A loud murmur of agreement.

"You do?" I whimper. "How did you—I mean—they're *special.*"

Huge laugh. I wish I could fill my stand-up with laughs like that. "Where did you . . . ?"

Cascading, overlapping voices: "Campaign headquarters!" "Friends!" "Congressman's office!" "My boss!" "Church!" "School!" "They were giving 'em out for free at the car wash!"

Wow. Okay, so, wait. Everyone in this whole fucking crowd has purple tickets? *Everyone?* The entire million of us?

Kinda makes my purple tickets a little less, ah, special. I turn my head and check out the people who are crammed against me, those in my immediate area. I can see that a few of them are actually holding purple tickets right now and others have their hands stuffed inside their pockets, no doubt hanging onto purple tickets.

Breathe. Deep breaths. Ahhh. Again. Better.

New attitude.

I don't give a shit about everybody here having purple fucking tickets. As long as we get inside the Mall.

"Attention, please, purple ticket holders!"

Heavy metal voice crackling through a loudspeaker.

"I'm sorry to inform you that the purple section is now closed.

Even if you hold purple tickets, you will not be admitted. We are sorry for the inconvenience."

WHAT?????

Sorry for the *inconvenience*?

You must be kidding me.

"Fuck," I say. "I can't believe this."

Even though I speak aloud, my voice is drowned out in the din.

I turn to a man next to me. He is older, African-American, bundled up in a long overcoat. Beneath the coat he is wearing a suit and tie. He holds an American flag.

"I rode the bus up from Florida," he says. "Waited my whole life for this. I can't be shut out."

Then, almost in slow motion, the crowd begins to move together, first plowing forward, as if we need to get a better look at the Purple Gate to make sure it's closed. Then, as if we're all part of a massive Chinese fire drill, we disperse, frantically, confused, trying to regroup, find our bearings.

Some people follow the largest remaining section of the crowd down the street into a tunnel. This strikes me as insane. Turns out I'm right. This tunnel will eventually be featured in news reports and blogs, renamed the Purple Tunnel of Doom. Purple ticket holders will file inside the tunnel and be stopped, stuck, crammed inside for the entire inaugural ceremony, no bathrooms, food, water, unable to move, trapped, like they're in some end-of-the-world disaster movie.

So, no, I'm not going into any tunnel. I'm not sure where I am gonna go. But I'm gonna get inside that Mall and get into that inauguration if I have to climb that fucking fence. I stand frozen in place for a second, figuring my next move, when someone shouts, "Over here!"

There is urgency in that voice. I like that. Because things right now are reaching stage critical. I will go with urgent as opposed to unsure, or what I'm feeling right now, clueless. I follow that voice, which has come from a group of about fifty people who are moving the opposite way—away from the Mall. I jog behind the group, then slowly move up through the pack until I'm close to the front. We cut to the left and veer back toward the Mall. We follow the line of the fence, slowing down, walking now, farther away from the Purple Gate, away from the crowd.

One guy, presumably the owner of the urgent voice, seems to be in charge. He's a young guy in a long camel coat. He stops suddenly. He has found a slight tear at the bottom of the fence. Looking around to make sure there are no cops, he starts to pull at the small opening of the fencing. Two more people kneel down next to him and start yanking at the fencing. After a few minutes, they wrest the fencing up, stretching out the hole they've created. They yank again and pull, and finally, they make a hole wide enough to fit a person.

One by one, people step through the hole in the fence and onto the Mall grounds. My turn.

"Purple tickets, my ass," I say. The people around me laugh. I bend over, and, like that dude in *Prison Break,* I snake through the opening, and then—

Freedom!

I don't believe this. I got fucking tickets and I still have to sneak into this shit.

But I'm in!

I look around crazily, and now, more clueless than ever, I just keep going, following the guy in the camel coat, who is moving with purpose, heading right to the purple section, where I am supposed to be in the first place.

I don't want anything special anymore. I just want to see Barack Obama become president. Is that too much to ask?

I look at my watch.

10:43 a.m.

I sprint in and out of people rushing, a few people swelling now from a small swarm into a throng, and then *wham*, I am swept into what has grown into a sea of humanity. It happens instantly. One second I'm through the fence, on the grounds, I'm *in . . .* and the next second I'm swamped, crushed again!

But I see, crazily, that I'm kind of close to the stage. Or what I think is the stage, or the podium, or at least part of the podium on the steps of the Capitol building where Barack Obama will be sworn in.

The reason I'm not sure is that I am blocked by a huge tree.

I can see to my right and to my left. Sort of. If I stretch as far as I can. Because this is no ordinary tree. This is the Shaquille O'Neal of trees. Even though it's winter and the branches of the tree are bare, leafless, I still can't see around the motherfucker. And forget moving so I can get a better view. I am now stopped. Jammed in tight. Crushed. This is my position for the next hour. This is where I will be.

"I just wanted to get to the purple section," I say miserably.

"You're in it," the woman next to me says.

"I am?"

"I have purple tickets," the woman says.

"They locked out everybody who had purple tickets," a heavyset woman on the other side of me says. "How did you get in?"

"I've been here all night," the first woman says.

"I was talking to *him*," the second woman says.

"I squeezed in under the fence. Crawled in on my belly like a commando," I say, and both women laugh. I hold for a second and laugh with them. What the hell.

"This is like Woodstock," the first woman says.

"Were you there?" number two says.

"No," the first woman admits.

"I was," the second woman says, and sniffs. "This is nothing like Woodstock. Woodstock was hot, rainy, muddy. We were all nude."

I feel my eyebrow rise. The woman glares at me. "That's right, honey," she says. "I was nude. All of me. High and butt negged. The worst part? I went to the bathroom, came back, and somebody stole our tent and all my clothes. So then I was *nude* nude because I didn't have any clothes to put on even if I wanted to. The stage was tiny. We were miles away. I couldn't see anything. It was not a good experience."

"Did you see Hendrix?" I ask her.

"Nope. Someone handed me some clothes, so we left before he came on. Nothing went right."

"This will be better," I say. "It has to be."

"It already is," she says. "It already is."

For the next forty-five minutes or so, the people around me push against me, crush me, pin me, fall against me, bump into me, slam into me, lean into me. I'm pressed up against the people around me, jostled, slammed, feet aching, uncomfortable, should have used the bathroom an hour ago, mashed, smashed, feeling as if I'm a sandwich spread and everyone else is the bread.

Then I hear a voice inside me saying, *This is fucked up. You're standing with a million people, all strangers, blocked by this big motherfucking tree, flew all this way, paid all this money, got the purple tickets, lost the purple tickets, found the purple tickets, lost your wife, can't see shit, you should be angry, dude, rip-shit pissed off, kick-some-ass* angry!

But I'm not.

There is no anger here. There is just no anger anywhere. Not today. I believe that I feel what everyone else feels.

Just glad to be here. It is that simple. It feels like a blessing. The joy that permeated the air last night is still here, hovering over us all like a contact high. That's what I'm feeling. The residue. The residue of joy. Still crackling in the air.

Spaced around the Mall at intervals are a few select Jumbotron TV screens that will project the inauguration to the entire crowd, including all of the pre-ceremony events—Aretha Franklin's song, Rick Warren's prayer, the swearing in of the vice president, President Barack Obama's oath of office, his acceptance speech, and Elizabeth Alexander's poem. Apparently, from the buzz I'm hearing around me, there is a big huge giant motherfucking jumbo Jumbotron right in front of us.

I wouldn't know. I can't see it.

It's also blocked by the tree.

What kind of fucking tree is this?

It looks like a huge, super-gi-normous, monster tree, but instead of branches it has enormous ugly wood tentacles. It's big enough to blot out the sun.

I'm still not angry.

Feeling good. Feeling calm. Feeling all stoked up.

I see this now as a kind of spiritual test. Almost biblical. Or maybe it's simply a testament to Barack Obama.

"I'm telling you, he can make a blind man see."

That's exactly how I feel.

Too much? Too over the top? Too messianic? Too larger-than-life?

Well, I'm sorry. Given where we've been and where we have to go, we need a president that is far from ordinary.

✳ ✳ ✳

Later, historians will call this day "The Moment."

I will call it "Feelings."

Because I can't see shit—except for this tree—but I feel. And I hear.

It starts at 11:28 a.m.

A voice from a loudspeaker announces, "Ladies and gentlemen . . . Laura Bush and Lynne Cheney!"

A smattering of applause as the soon-to-be former First Lady and Mrs. Dr. Evil make their way out of the rotunda of the Capitol to their seats. Don't really care if I see them or not.

11:31 a.m.

Michelle Obama and Jill Biden!

Huge applause. I stretch my neck. Stand on my toes. Repress the urge to climb on top of the guy next to me. Crane my neck again. Can't see a thing. Get in touch with my feelings. Okay. I'm experiencing this. Feels good. Feels great.

I suddenly remember I have to do an interview. I promised to call my friend Adam Carolla's radio show and do a report from the inauguration, live. I hit his number on my cell, and within seconds I'm on the air.

"Hey, DAG, how's it going?"

"What?" I yell into the phone.

"How is it going?"

"I can barely hear you. And I can't see anything."

"What?"

Frustrated, I scream, "I CAN'T SEE SHIT!"

The phone goes dead.

✳   ✳   ✳

11:36 a.m.

George Bush.

Nothing. Barely polite applause. Actually more like an icy silence. I don't stretch. Don't care if I can't see. Over the last eight years, I've seen enough.

Then behind Bush—as I will later see on the inauguration replay and endless updates and on late-night television talk shows—all dressed in black, Dick Cheney rolls up in a wheelchair. He looks like Dr. Strangelove. In one hand he holds a cane. I'm sure that inside the cane he keeps a sword dipped in rat poison. He rolls up, an evil grin slapped on his face. All that's missing is the demented cackle.

11:38 a.m.

Vice President–elect Joe Biden.

Bounds down the stairs to thunderous applause. He grins, waves. The applause builds as the Democratic leadership gathers behind him.

11:43 a.m.

Nancy Pelosi, Harry Reid head down the steps. Crowd is cheering wildly.

I can't see a thing, but I'm overwhelmed by a feeling of anticipation. Feel it coursing through me like a jolt of electricity.

11:45 a.m.

More Democrats. Senator Dianne Feinstein, chair of the Joint Congressional Committee on Inaugural Ceremonies, walks slowly down the steps. She will host the proceedings. Applause mixed with anticipation as Senator Feinstein steps up to the microphone. She pauses for half a second and introduces Barack Obama.

Loud, raucous applause that rises into a frenzy. And then—

Insanity.

Out of control, fever-pitched INSANITY.

I cannot see Barack Obama—I can't see anything—but I feel swept away by the emotion. I turn and look behind me, and I see literally two miles of people, an ocean of faces that stretches from the Washington Monument to the Lincoln Memorial. It seems as if every person here—all two million—is waving a flag. What results is an undulating, two-mile, red, white, and blue tsunami. The roar continues nonstop, like a thunderous, echoing waterfall.

I'm here to bear witness, I say to myself.

This is my lesson. My duty. I'm a blind witness, relying on all of my other senses. But being present at The Moment is bigger than being able to see. In the place, on this spot, unable to see, I am still part of this incredible *feeling.* I experience the passion of the moment. The elation. It is shared by this mile of two million people. It is profound. And deeply, innately uplifting.

I'm not sure how long it takes the applause to fade out—a full minute, two, three—I can't be sure. But eventually Senator Feinstein manages to introduce Rick Warren, the controversial pastor of the Saddleback Church in Lake Forest, California, who will deliver the invocation. Pastor Warren makes his way to the microphone.

A middle-aged black woman, who, appropriately at this moment, is dressed for church, appears at my side. She must have been here all along, but I haven't noticed her. She looks up at me, her eyes narrowing, as if she is contemplating something, perhaps about to make a decision. Then she speaks to me, slowly, softly, measuring her words.

"I can't find my family," she says.

"Excuse me?" I say.

"I've lost my family."

Man, I think. *This is a sad story. I feel horrible. But does she have to tell me this now? During all this joy?*

"That's terrible," I say. "I'm very sorry for your loss."

"Oh, no. They're alive. I've just *lost* them. My husband, my sons. We were all together, but now I don't know where they're at. They're gone."

"I know what you mean," I say. "I lost my family, too."

Her bottom lip quivers. "Would you be my family?"

I look at her. Her eyes have filled with tears.

"Absolutely," I say.

She smiles up at me and grabs my hand with both of hers. We silently bow our heads as Rick Warren begins his benediction. My eyes fill as he prays for us, for our country, and for President Barack

Obama. He asks that God help us become "united in our commitment to freedom." Amen.

Aretha Franklin appears next. Later, when I watch the replay I'll see that she is wearing the biggest hat in the history of headwear. The thing fills up the Jumbotron. Frankly, I have mixed feelings about it. Either her hat is audacious and magnificent and she has started a fashion trend in the same way President Kennedy ended a fashion trend by not wearing a hat at his inauguration, or she is balancing a gray velvet boat on her head.

Before I make my decision, Aretha launches into "My Country 'Tis of Thee." There is nothing ambiguous here. The Queen of Soul still has chops. She knocks that motherfucker out of the Mall. If you aren't on your feet while Barack Obama walks down the Capitol steps, then you are probably a Republican. But if you aren't on your feet while Aretha sings "My Country 'Tis of Thee," then you are probably dead.

After Aretha tears it up, Justice Stevens swears in our new vice president, Joe Biden. To show you how completely that tree blocks my view, I can't even see his teeth.

Another extraordinary musical moment follows. A quartet made up of Yo-Yo Ma, Itzhak Perlman, Anthony McGill, and Gabriela Montero performs. Dazzling. This time I just close my eyes and let the music pick me up and take me away. Because music is meant to be heard. And I do *hear* this. I gotta say, as good as Aretha was, these four soar.

Then the moment of The Moment.

The swearing in of #44, Barack Obama. The chief justice—in this case Justice John Roberts—traditionally administers the oath of office. As I am made aware by people around me doing play-by-play, Michelle Obama hands the Lincoln Bible, an enormous pale gold volume, to Justice Roberts, who holds it while Barack Obama rests his right hand on the top.

The woman next to me, my new family, squeezes my hand. Then she begins to cry. I reach my arms around her and hug her. She sniffles and cries louder.

"It's okay," I say. I close my eyes and begin patting her on the back.

As I rub her back, my hands bump into another pair of hands—not belonging to me. I open my eyes and I see that another woman, sitting in a folding chair slightly behind my new cousin, is circling her hands on my cousin's back.

"It's all right," the seated woman says. "Shhh."

"Hey," I say, catching the seated woman's eye. I give her a shrug, a subtle signal that I hope she can read, because I'm saying, in that shrug, "*What the fuck are you doing?*"

"I'll be your family, too," the woman in the folding chair says, an edge of defiance in her voice.

My new family just nods and sobs louder.

"Really?" I say to the woman in the folding chair. "You think she needs more than one family at the inauguration? I can handle this. I'm big enough to be her whole family all by myself."

"Shhh," the woman in the folding chair says, rubbing my cousin's back, kneading it with her knuckles, as if she has suddenly become a masseuse.

I nod at her. "So you're gonna horn in on this? You're gonna horn in on my new family?"

The woman in the folding chair ignores me. Or doesn't hear me. She just keeps on rubbing.

Now, I want to be absolutely clear. I am not angry. Not at all. Not even remotely close to feeling angry. There is no anger here today. None. Whatsoever.

And that amazes me.

But, I'm telling you, I have the consoling and back rubbing under control. I am taking care of business. Why does this woman feel the need to kick me out of the way? Am I a lousy consoler? Am I bad at back rubbing? Is this some kind of weird inaugural threesome that I fell into? My middle-aged cousin, a woman in a folding chair, and me? It's as if the woman in the folding chair has become our pushy in-law. The deadbeat. The one who shows up at the most inappropriate times, or just before dinner. Feels kind of fucked-up.

I'm not gonna let her steal my new family.

I start rubbing my new family's back, harder. It works. The woman in the folding chair backs off.

At the podium, remaining cool, despite Justice Roberts's flubbing of the words, Barack Obama completes the presidential oath of office, and the frenzy, the insanity, the JOY resumes. My new cousin starts bawling, and I return to rubbing her back. Around us, behind us, in front of us, two million people wave their American flags, while cheering their lungs out, and somewhere close by a cannon blasts. Barack Obama steps to the microphone and, after literally one solid minute of applause and cheering, begins his acceptance speech. His words are solemn, strong, and stirring. When he finishes delivering his speech, more applauding and cheering erupt, but this time there is a slight tinge of sobriety in the air, a whiff, because at last the wait is over. Barack Obama is in. The "elect" in *president-elect* has been excised; he is now officially President Barack Obama. I have born witness to history. I have *heard* history in the making.

To put a cap on the proceedings, Elizabeth Alexander, President Obama's choice as inaugural poet, approaches the podium, adjusts the microphone. She begins to read a poem she's written especially for the occasion. I bow my head to listen. When I lift my head about five seconds later, I'm the only one left in my area. My new cousin is gone. The woman and her folding chair are gone. The entire purple section is virtually empty. It has happened in the blink of an eye. All the people who seconds ago stood crammed against each other—people wearing people—now stream for the exits. It's stunning. At least I've just learned a valuable survival tip, which I will now pass on to you.

If you ever want to get people to vacate an area—say you're having a dinner party, it's getting late, they're lying around all over, and you want them to get the hell out—just read them a poem.

✶   ✶   ✶

With no offense meant to Elizabeth Alexander, whom I can't see anyway behind this enormous giant cartoon tree, I start to leave. I turn away from the Capitol, take two steps, and stop.

A thought occurs to me.

I'm standing here in the purple section. I have just heard the historic inauguration of Barack Obama. It was mind-blowing, moving beyond words, something I can't wait to tell Luisa about when she gets older and pass on someday to my grandkids. Hard to picture myself with grandkids, since Luisa just turned one and has only recently learned to identify her feet. Still . . .

I stop because there is something gnawing at me. Something I need to do.

I need to see the VIP platinum seats.

I need to see what I almost had. Or thought I almost had. How much better can they be?

I walk past the tree and head in a direct line to the podium, where Elizabeth Alexander finishes reading her poem to strong applause from the twelve people who are left, probably her relatives. Can't tell if the poem is any good or if I'm hearing mercy clapping. Haven't really been listening. I am on a mission. I need to see these damn VIP platinum seats.

I walk another ten feet and stop. I'm here. Standing at the edge of the platinum section. It's true. These seats are really good. Primo. Dead center. Facing the podium, or slightly off to the left and right. Either way, the seats are close. Plus, they are actually *seats*. No standing area. And not just chairs. Padded chairs. You would have to call the platinum section the VIPest of the VIP seats. Exclusive. Probably unattainable. This is the section that you stare at with envy at every concert or event, right in front of the stage, and you always turn to the person you're with and say, "Look at those seats. Right down in front. Who are those people? How did they get those seats? They either know somebody or have too much money. Man. Someday I'm gonna sit in those seats."

But I know the score. I know who those people are. We're talking about very famous people like Denzel and Spike Lee and Mohammad Ali and . . . *MC Hammer*???

Are you shitting me?

Wait a minute. That can't be MC Hammer.

I move up to get a closer look.

It *is* MC Hammer!

Hasn't he been broke since like 1997? Isn't he over? How the fuck did MC Hammer score a VIP platinum premium ticket and I had to stand crushed against a million strangers rubbing a stranger's back?

I guess the MC stands for "More Clout."

* * *

As the immortal bard Willie Shakespeare said, "All's well that ends well."

After the inauguration, I walk back to the hotel. The whole way I feel as if I'm floating, caught up in an altered state of blissfulness. As I walk, all around me I feel the residue of joy, as someone calls it, like a kind of mist that has fallen, blanketing the entire city.

President Barack Obama.

Sure has a nice ring to it. It's musical, powerful, hopeful, and I am grateful.

I hit the hotel lobby and find Christine waiting for me. We run into each other's arms and hold each other as if we've been apart for a week. We then go to lunch and break down our mornings. We've had similar experiences. She saw more than I did—not hard, since I saw nothing. By the time we return to our room, we have to get dressed for the inaugural ball that we will attend. As everyone I know has strongly suggested, I've hired a limo to take us to the ball. Without a car, they say, we'll be totally screwed. The town will be shut down, the streets will be jammed, and it will take hours to get back and forth to the ball. Good advice. We get into our limo—which costs $1,500 for the night—and settle in for the ride. The limo drives for about three minutes, stops, and the driver comes around and opens the door. We've arrived at our ball, which is being held two blocks from the hotel. Good move, DAG. Talk about $1,500 well spent.

But am I angry? Hell, no! Not tonight. I feel giddy.

We sleep late the next morning and take the afternoon to sightsee. The morning after that, we check out of the hotel early and return to Los Angeles. I'm going to attend a postelection party Saturday night, the bookend to the Century City election party I hosted. By Saturday, four days into Barack Obama's presidency, I'm astonished by the media coverage. It's out of control.

"Hi, this is Charlie Wallace on CNN, covering the Barack Obama presidency, Minute 1,537. I can report that President Obama spent this minute answering e-mails on his BlackBerry and reading a briefing of some kind that was handed to him by a member of his staff. He read the briefing carefully, nodding occasionally. Now let's go to Heather Lee, who will bring you the details of the Obama presidency, Minute 1,538."

"Thank you, Charlie."

"Heather, I believe that President Obama may be standing up during this Presidential Minute."

"That's right, Charlie. There he goes! He is getting to his feet. And, oh my, look, he is flattening his tie. I can't tell whether his flattening of the tie was a reflex or whether it was planned."

"Hard to tell from this angle, Heather."

"Well, to analyze the significance of his tie flattening and to determine whether it was a reflex, or planned, and if so, who planned it, let's go to the best political team on television, David Gergen, Jeffrey Toobin, Campbell Brown, Roland Martin, and John King, who has blown up the tie onto a large touch screen and will go over which patterns were flattened, which were ignored, and why."

CAN WE PLEASE LEAVE HIM ALONE?

✳ ✳ ✳

Saturday night. A ballroom jammed with some of L.A.'s best and brightest. All feeling high and happy and full of hope. People swirl by me. We exchange inauguration stories. Everyone here got at least a glimpse of the president. Everyone but me. It honestly doesn't matter. I was there. About an hour into the party, after I graze along the buffet table, an older couple tracks me down.

"David Alan Grier," the man says. "I saw you at the election party in Century City."

"That was quite a night," I say.

"Oh, yeah. That was really something."

"I couldn't go," his wife says. "I had a procedure the next day. What happened?"

"I was the host," I say modestly.

I lower my head, brace myself for a compliment. I feel a smile form.

"It was unbelievable," the man says. "David Alan Grier. He starts crying. Bawling like a baby."

My smile freezes.

"Totally breaks down," the old dude says. "Sobbing. In front of everyone—"

Please, I shout inside. *Do you really have to do this?*

The guy won't stop. "Must've been a thousand people. And he's sobbing. It was like he was naked."

"I was, you know, moved," I mumble.

"Embarrassing," the man says. "You never saw anything like it. He was just bawling."

"I wish I could've seen that," his wife says.

No, you don't, I say to myself.

✳   ✳   ✳   **14**   ✳   ✳   ✳

THE SEVENTY-TWO-HOUR RULE

October 3, 2008.

My show, my baby, *Chocolate News*, premieres. The studio audience howls, and the show receives some of the best reviews of my career. The *Washington Post, Boston Globe,* and *New York Post* rave, and the dude in the *Hollywood Reporter,* one of the two top show-business trade papers, goes nuts. He says the show ". . . delivers with irreverent muscle . . ." and calls me "the funniest dude living in the world right now."

I'm hot! I stand up a little bit taller now when I'm buying diapers at the market and pulling the trash bins down to the curb. I notice that the guard at the studio lot smiles at me now instead of searching my trunk before he lets me through the gate. I start getting calls to appear on other shows wanting to book me as a guest. Makes them look good having a hot TV star like me instead of some washed-up has-been. But because I'm officially *sizzling*, I can pick and choose.

For example.

Dancing with the Stars calls.

My reaction?

ARE YOU OUT OF YOUR DAMN MIND?

I am not doing some bullshit reality show. Fuck you. Okay? I have a career. I can actually act. And perform. And create topical material every damn week. Have you not read these reviews? Motherfucker. Kiss my ass. Read my lips. N-O.

They call again.

"You know, David, we really would love to have you. Think about it."

I'm huffy as hell. "Excuse me, brother. People are talking Emmy for *Chocolate News*, okay? Em-me. You hear me? I don't need this bullshit. Don't call me back. I'm offended."

They won't quit. They try a third time. But this time they get cagey. They hit me where I live. They enlist two of my friends to sell me.

First, comedian Jeff Ross, who appeared on the show and got voted off the first week, calls.

"The producers asked me to call you," Jeff says. "They love you. They would be honored if you did the show. Can I tell you something? It is the best, most incredible experience. And I got knocked off the first week. But I swear, DAG, it's wonderful."

"What's so wonderful about it?"

"You're dancing with hot chicks. They're all around you. The money is great. And—" He lowers his voice. "My road price went up."

Now he's hit home.

"Your road fee went up?"

"Like double. Even triple."

Okay, he's got my attention.

Then my close friend Adam Carolla, another *Dancing with the Stars* alumnus, who lasted four weeks, calls to seal the deal.

"DAG, you've got to do it."

"Awright, why?"

"Let me see if I can explain this. It's deep. Okay. You're backstage and you're waiting to perform your paso doble. Suddenly, you hear the roar of America and an enormous rush goes through you. It's indescribable."

I wait.

"You're kidding me, right?"

"I am not kidding you," Adam says. "You get this feeling of power. And you experience this *thrill*. You look at your partner and you think, *I have ninety pounds of blonde beauty on my arm and I am about to turn this country on its ear.*"

He's gone, I think. *He's lost his mind. He actually believes this shit.*

"It's a spiritual experience," Adam says.

"I'll think about it," I say.

"Plus I lost thirty pounds."

Doubling my road fee. Dropping thirty pounds. These guys are good. They make it sound tempting. But I pass.

✳ ✳ ✳

February 3, 2009.

Four months to the day of the *Chocolate News* premiere.

I celebrate by having a colonoscopy. When I return from the procedure—dazed, blurry-eyed, fuzzy-headed, walking like John Wayne—my manager hits me on my cell.

"David, are you sitting down?"

"Not yet. Not until I experience at least a five-minute fart. Then I'll be able to sit down. Why?"

"I have some bad news."

I draw myself up. "Just give it to me. Give it to me straight. I'll take it on the chin."

"*Chocolate News* has been canceled."

I feel like I've been hit by a train.

"Okay," I say. Which is all I manage to get out. My heart is thumping.

"Are you all right?"

"Nah, I'm cool. These things happen. I mean, of course I'm disappointed."

"Purely a business decision," my manager says.

"Oh, no, I hear that. Look, I'm not a kid. I've been around. This shit goes with the territory. It's a miracle any show gets picked up. You got to have a good attitude and move on."

"That's very mature."

"I am surprised. I have to say that. In this political climate, you'd think that a show like *Chocolate News* would have had a shot. That they might have stuck with it."

"It was a tough call."

"Well. It is what it is. Okay. Move on. That's what we have to do."

"All we can do."

"I've been here before. Many, many times. Seen more than my share of canceled shows. This is nothing new. I feel like a gang member who's been shot for the eleventh time. I know the feeling."

"You sure you're all right?"

"Nah, I'm cool. Moving on."

"You're taking this awfully well."

"That's how I do. I've been through the wars, man. Ain't no big thing."

"All right then. I'll talk to you later."

"*Next,*" I say cheerfully. "That's my motto."

I hang up, feeling as if I've taken it up the ass twice in twelve hours.

✴   ✴   ✴

I have a seventy-two-hour rule.

When bad shit happens, I allow myself seventy-two hours to wallow. I give myself three days to feel depressed, angry, worthless, sorry for myself, and a total piece of shit. After three days—seventy-two hours—I shake it off, hop right back on the horse, come back strong.

Not this time.

Two weeks after I get the news, I'm still wallowing. I'm still sitting in my robe, unshaven, immobile, a cranky, self-pitying mess.

"What is wrong with you?" Christine asks me in the middle of week three.

"They stole my show!" I wail. "Those motherfuckers stole my show!"

"David—"

"Why did they do it? *Why? WHY?* Christine, I'm having a breakdown. Bring me pills. I don't care what kind. Bring me a bucket of PILLS!"

Christine rolls her eyes and leaves. I picture myself still sitting here in my bathrobe five years from now. I have a beard down to the floor and I can't fucking move because—

THEY STOLE MY SHOW!!!!!

And then I really hit bottom.

Beeep.

A voice mail.

"Hi, DAG, how are you?" a voice coos. It's that female exec from Comedy Central I used to flirt with all the time. "I'm sorry I haven't called you before this. Life, you know? Anyway. There are so many things I want to discuss with you. First and foremost is that you are wildly, wildly talented, and kind, and lovely, and sexy, that's off the record. And so motherfuckin' funny. There are moments on *Chocolate News,* so many characters and laughs that are my favorite, favorite things that I've seen since I've worked here. I only wish that I could have been closer to it, and closer to you. So I want to talk to you about that. And, two, I want to find out how your family is, and the baby. And, three, I have something that I think you might be interested in doing and that I would love you to do. And that is . . . to be on the dais for the Larry the Cable Guy roast. Larry has said, 'I really, really, really would love to have DAG.' So I want to find out if you'll do it. I think you would kill. And I think it's big. They're bold. They're pretty hip. I don't know. Maybe it could be fun? So those are the three things I want to talk to you about. Call me at your leisure. I love you. Bye."

Okay.

The Larry the Cable Guy roast?

In two weeks I have gone from creator, executive producer, writer, performer, and host of *Chocolate News* to roasting Larry the Cable Guy? We're back to that? *Git 'er done!* And *You know you're a redneck if . . . ?* What happened to from nada to Prada, from hoochie to Gucci, from the jail cell to Chanel, if it's chocolate, I'll bring it to you? What about the Chocolate-Covered Truth?

Forget Blue Collar. There is no more black *anything.*

Right now the blackest thing on Comedy Central is the dildo shoved up Lisa Lampanelli's ass.

I listen to the message again.

Then I call my manager.

"So glad to hear from you, DAG," he says. "What's up?"

"I don't care what it takes," I say. "I don't care who you have to kill, who you have to pay off, or who you have to fuck, but get me on *Dancing with the Stars.*"

It's a done deal. I'm invited to join the cast of *Dancing with the Stars, 2009.* What's weird is I'm actually excited about it. I check my competition. Among them are rapper Lil' Kim (I know her!); Shawn Johnson, Olympic gold medalist who's about twelve; Gilles Marini, the naked dude from the *Sex and the City* movie, which I'm proud to say I have not seen, thus validating my manliness; Ty Murray, rodeo star (never heard of him) and his wife, Jewel (heard of her); Steve-O from *Jackass,* who literally stapled his nut sack together (how good a dancer could he be?); Steve Wozniak, cofounder of Apple Computer (maybe if I'm nice to him I can score a new iPhone); and Lawrence Taylor, only the greatest, most feared, hardest-hitting football player who ever lived. Note to self: Do not dis LT's dancing.

At breakfast, I go over my competition with Christine.

"This will be kind of fun," she says, going over the list.

I stare at her. "Fun? Are you kidding me? This is war. I'm gonna win this thing. If I have to, I will play dirty. I'm gonna do anything it takes. These people are going down."

I study the list of names over Christine's shoulder. "Shawn Johnson. Olympic gold medal winner. Going down. She's four feet tall. Walks like a robot. Going *down.*"

Christine rolls her eyes. I slap another name on the list. "Steve-O. The *Jackass* dude. Just got out of rehab. I'm gonna send him some coke. Get him some cocaine. Same with LT. Get these two to have a relapse. Ty Murray, the rodeo dude? Gonna let three or four bulls loose in his dressing room. Let them gore his ass. These people are going down!"

Christine shakes her head. "Who is your partner?"

"She's Brazilian, very young, very sexually open."

The laser stare.

"I don't know who it is. They haven't told us yet."

"Well." My wife sips her coffee. "As long as you agreed to do it, and since it's the biggest television show in America, you'd better win."

I stare at her. "I was playing before. Kidding. I just can't have fun?"

She looks at me as if I'm high.

"No," she says finally. "You have to win."

＊　＊　＊

That afternoon I'm in Beverly Hills at a jewelry store buying some bracelets and trinkets and stuff for Christine. Hanging at the jewelry counter. Gasping at the prices.

I hear some whispering coming from the other end of the store. "I'm telling you, that's him."

A salesclerk, an older Jewish woman, approaches me.

"Excuse me," she says. "David Alan Grier, right? From TV."

I smile. "That's right. *In Living Color* and—"

A catch in my throat.

"—*Chocolate News.*"

She looks at me blankly. "Don't know those." Her face lights up. "But I see you're on *Dancing with the Stars.*"

"Oh, yes, that's right."

"That show I love."

"Really?"

The little voice of reason inside my head is flashing a warning: *Get out. Go. Get out of this store now. GO.*

"So?" she says, eyebrows rising.

"Uh. Yes?"

"Show me how to dance."

I laugh. She doesn't. She's serious.

"I used to be a wonderful dancer," she says. "At the USO. My specialty was the waltz. That's how I landed my husband. Anyway. There's always a waltz on *Dancing with the Stars.* You know how to waltz?"

"Well, yeah, I—"

She throws her arms around me and we begin to waltz in front of the jewelry counter. I resist for about two seconds—then, what the hell, I give in—and I gently waltz her past the jewelry counter and all around the store. The salesclerks—mostly elderly Jewish women—drop what they're doing and start clapping. One of them squeezes out from behind the counter, steps up to us, taps my partner on the shoulder, and cuts in.

"Get away, Gladys," my partner says, spinning us away from her. "He's mine!"

Roaring from the salesclerks, including two black chicks, who are clapping in rhythm.

"Go, honey, go!" the first one shouts.

"You better win that competition, boo boo," the other one says.

Damn.

What pressure.

✳   ✳   ✳

I hear through the grapevine that all the other "stars" are actually taking this cheesy dance show seriously. I'm not obsessive—well, okay, maybe a little bit—but I think I'd better protect my ass. I hire a webmaster and an internet PR firm and tell them to help me out because I will be MySpacing, Facebooking, blogging, video blogging, Flogging, texting, Twittering, and Tweaking. I also talk to a friend, a trainer, and tell him I want to put in some extra work. I'm not about to look like an out-of-shape buffoon in front of 20 million people.

"Why do you want to change your routine?" my friend, the trainer, asks. "You in a movie?"

"No. I'm doing *Dancing with the Stars.*"

He looks at me with deep concern, as if I've just told him I've joined the Marines and I'm about to be shipped to Afghanistan.

"You have to talk to my doctor," he says.

"Why?"

"DAG, you *need* to talk to my doctor."

Did he just wink?

"Trust me."

There it is again.

"Okay. I'll do it. I'm definitely interested in building a better me."

"He's your man. Call him today."

I want to say, on the record, that this doctor—call him Dr. X—is a legitimate doctor, and that everything I do during *Dancing with the Stars* is perfectly legal. It may not be legal if I'm trying to win the Tour de France or play for the New York Yankees, but hey.

I meet Dr. X the next afternoon.

"I hear there is some urgency," Dr. X says. "What can I do for you?"

"I'm going on *Dancing with the Stars,*" I say.

"Oh, my God," Dr. X says. "You are going to need the A-level, full-boost regimen."

I don't flinch. "Hit me up, Doc."

Here is what Dr. X prescribes:

Phentremine, 37.5 mg, half a tab, twice a day; glucosamine, 500 mg, 3 caps daily; chondroitin, 400 mg, 1 cap daily; vitamin B supreme, 1 cap daily; HGH, 4 shots, 5 days on, 2 days off; testosterone, liquid, 3 drops, 2 times a day; DHEA, 25 mg, 1 cap daily; resveratrol Synergy, 200 mg, 1 cap daily; DFH complex multivitamin, 6 caps daily; Endotrim, 2 caps daily; PaleoMeal-DF and Meal Replacement Protein shake.

I nod at the prescription, figure I may as well go for broke.

"This takes care of the lower forty. Now, what about my hair?"

Dr. X sends me to his friend, Dr. Z, the dermatologist. Dr. Z zaps me with Botox and Restylane. I dye my hair every four days, fill in the thinning spots with some hair flecking shit, and spray my whole head with liquid hair holder. My hair is growing and holding. I could be hit in the head by a tornado and my hair won't budge.

I tell no one. Don't tell my friends. Do not tell my wife. I want no hassles, do not want to take the chance that I will be busted. I'm careful, make sure nobody sees my routine. I sneak my shit in the garage. I store my stash in the refrigerator out there. I keep my eye on the clock, then when it's time, I announce that I have to feed the dogs. I dash into the garage, take out my stuff, double back around, sneak into the guest bathroom, shoot up my HGH, throw down my seven or eight horse pills, return the remaining stuff to the fridge in the garage, and head back inside, waiting for the ride to start. I do this three times a day for a week.

I feel nothing. Except a little jittery.

I return to Dr. X. He checks my levels. He looks grim. "You're on *Dancing with the Stars,* huh?"

My leg's bouncing a million miles an hour. "That's right. Starting my first rehearsal in a couple days. Two days. Not tomorrow. The next day. Just two days."

"That show's a killer. I'm gonna boost you up."

"I'm with you. I am with *you*."

Does the extra dosage make any difference?

Let's just say that when I stroll into the rehearsal hall that first day, I feel . . . supremely . . . *confident.*

15

DWTS DIARY

Even though Christine says I have to win, and the black chicks and the old Jewish ladies in the jewelry store say I have to win, I don't give a shit if I win. The show is a joke, a silly reality show, and I am not taking it seriously. I'm here to have fun. Period.

First day of rehearsal.

I walk into the dance studio. Immediately, someone slaps a microphone on me, the cameras start rolling, and the show starts. One of the producers leads me toward a gorgeous blonde beauty.

"We mike everybody up first day and put a camera on you," the producer says in a British accent. "We want to catch you coming in to meet your dance partner. Are you all right with that?"

"Well, I guess—"

"And . . . *action!* Here we are. David Alan Grier, this is Kym Johnson."

Kym—hot, blonde, Australian, and have I mentioned *HOT?*—extends a long, thin arm.

In less than the time it takes to blink, I consider my options. How to play this?

Two choices.

The "Oh my God, you are so gorgeous. It is a pleasure to meet you" way.

Or the DAG way.

I go DAG.

I check her out like she's sending off a slightly funky smell.

"Okay, first of all," I say, "I hate blondes. And, honey, you have a fat ass. You gotta lose some *weight.*"

Her mouth opens, closes, opens, and stays there.

"What?" she says.

"Honey, what is your name?"

"Kym."

"Uh-huh. Now, Kym, what did you come in last year?"

"Second. I came in second place."

"Okay, that's the loser. You know what? I need you to dye your hair. 'Cuz you're telling the world, 'Hey, world, the loser in me is dead. This is the winner me.' Something in red. I think that would work."

"I don't really want to dye my hair—"

"Hey, I'm just thinking of you. Trying to help you out. And if you don't want to do it for you, do it for me. You go red, we're not dead."

She's looking at me, blinking furiously, speechless.

"Kym, there is no pressure here. Win, lose, I don't care. I just wanna lose some weight. Wanna walk out of here with a swimmer's body. Maybe score some free dance shoes. And, fingers crossed, sexual favors."

Later I hear she's in her dressing room, crying.

I find the producer, apologize, and say, "Look, how do you change partners? I messed up with Kym."

"You can't change partners. You have to stick with her."

I find Kym and apologize. Explain that I was fucking around. She says the words every comedian loves to hear: "I couldn't tell if you were joking or not."

Yeah. Love when you have to say, "These are *jokes.* Understand? Ha ha *ha*. Anyone?"

REHEARSAL

Kym forgives me. We're cool. I think. I still feel she's not too sure about me. What the fuck. This is going to be a hoot. I'll go on Adam Carolla's radio show and rag on the show, have some fun.

The old Jewish lady is right. The first dance is a waltz. Easy. I'm mugging for the camera, joking around, being an asshole. Fun.

About five minutes into rehearsal, I start to sweat.

Within fifteen minutes, I'm sweating as if I've just been falsely accused of a double murder. The sweat is shooting out of me like I got sprinkler heads buried in my flesh. I am dripping. Covering Kym with my sweat, too.

She doesn't seem to mind. She's a trouper. Crazily enough, I think she appreciates how hard I'm working.

She starts adding dance steps and a couple of simple moves. Simple to her. Complex as hell to me. I am having serious trouble learning this shit. Everything I do is off, wrong, screwed up. I can't get it. It's like I suddenly have hooves instead of feet.

And I am sore.

No, that's not correct.

I fucking *hurt.*

I feel as if I have been beaten with a stick and thrown out of a speeding Oldsmobile.

This goes on for days.

Every morning I get up and take a long, hot bath. I have morphed into my grandfather. I rub liniments all over my body. One day I spend twenty minutes in a drugstore next to three homeless guys staring at shelves of Bengay and Icy Hot. I buy everything. Then I get home and rub this stuff all over me with a roller. I pop Advil like Pez.

Then one day, the dance clicks. I pick up the steps. I start to feel fluid. Kym shows absolutely monklike patience putting up with me. I finally get it. I'm walking like a ninety-year-old man, I smell like Bengay, but having the dance work at last takes away some of the pain.

Although we're isolated in our rehearsal studio, separated from the other dancers, word about our competition starts to leak. We hear that Nancy O'Dell has seriously stepped it up and is rehearsing seven hours a day. I'm in disbelief.

"Seven hours a day? Are you serious?"

"I heard she's now up to eight hours," Kym says.

"I can barely go four hours. Even that's a stretch. Holy crap. She's out for blood."

The next day we hear that Nancy has ripped up her knee and is out of the competition. A few hours later, Jewel fractures the tibia in both her legs and joins Nancy on the sidelines. They are replaced by two reality TV stars: Holly Madison, the hot blonde from *The Girls Next Door,* known for posing for *Playboy* and telling the world that she wants to marry Hef and have his babies, and Melissa Rycroft, who stunningly got dumped on *The Bachelor,* the biggest show on ABC.

I break down our new competition to Kym. "Obviously, a business move. Melissa won the hearts of America when she got dumped, which means she's really popular and probably dances like Steve Wozniak. Holly? I know her and her titties. As does everyone. These two replacements do not worry me."

Midweek we show our dance to two of the producers, trailed as always by a cameraman. Kym and I kick it. We are on. We *kill* that waltz. The producers watch us, toes tapping, smiles flashing wide, applauding genuinely. They are clearly impressed. Bordering on dazzled.

"I have to tell you, in all seriousness, no bullshit," one of the producers says. "You guys are good."

A powerful, convincing statement. Made even more powerful and convincing when spoken in a British accent.

The second producer corners us and says in a quiet voice, "David and Kym, we've seen other couples. You didn't hear this from me, but"—he looks around—"they're not as good. You guys are *good.*"

As they head off to observe some of the lesser dancers, the cameraman makes it a point to pull Kym and me aside. "Can I tell you something? I've been with almost all the other couples. I can't tell you who. You guys are better than they are."

I dance out of that rehearsal hall on a fucking cloud. Honestly, I thought we were good, but now I *know* we're good. We are the team to beat.

The next morning Kym comes in with even more confirmation.

"I met the French guy, Gilles Marini."

"Who?"

"The guy from *Sex and the City*. You know, The Penis?"

"The what?"

"That's what every woman I know calls him. Oh, that's right, you haven't seen the movie."

"Not gonna, either. Why do they call him the—? Oh. Never mind."

"Anyway, trust me, David. He is not our competition."

"He may be a penis, Kym." I smile. "But we're good."

*   *   *

The week winds down. We're working hard, polishing our moves. I can't lie. I'm itching to see some of our competition.

We make a deal with Belinda Carlisle. She's in the rehearsal space down the hall. We'll show her ours, if she'll show us hers. We crack off our waltz. We dominate. Then she and her partner go into their waltz.

Horrible.

That's all I can say. Belinda, you are not good. Kym and I? Good. Very good. You and your partner? No good. Uh-uh.

I fly home so high I don't even need a car. I tell Christine, who eyes me now with some concern, "What can I say? I can win this. Why? Because we are good, Christine. We are very, very good. Now, I won't care if we come in second. That would be all right. Second place is nothing to sneeze at. You have to figure in the audience vote and unseen circumstances, all of that. So, first, second, either one is okay. I'll be right back."

"Where are you going?"

"Gotta feed the dogs."

If I go the distance and finish first or second, those dogs are gonna look like Clydesdales.

✶　✶　✶

Monday. Dress rehearsal. The first time we see all the dancers. I am standing as erect as a surfboard, feeling strong, confident, and a teeny bit jumpy from my juice. Just got an edge, that's all. Don't even need it, really, because we're good!

The first dancers to hit the floor are Gilles (The Penis) Marini and his partner, Cheryl. I'm not fazed. Kym said he's not our competition. I have to admit, though, the guy is handsome, ripped, and seems to move with ease and confidence. He's not good, though. We're good.

They dance and my world caves in. I lean over to Kym and whisper, "Holy shit. I thought you said he couldn't dance."

"I never actually saw him dance," she admits.

"We're screwed. This guy is Mikhail fucking Baryshnikov."

"Language," Kym says.

"French, I think. Holy fucking shit. Okay, we'll take second. Yeah, second. Second's all right."

Gilles and Cheryl complete their waltz and step up to three stand-in judges, who say wonderful things about them and all hold up 10s.

Melissa Rycroft—the *Bachelor* chick—and her partner take the floor next. I know she can't dance, so I relax. Wrong. She busts that waltz.

"Are you kidding me?" I ask Kym. "I've seen those moves before—at the New York City Ballet!"

"It's okay, David, we're good, too."

"We're double fucked. These two are ringers."

Shawn Johnson, Olympic gold medal winner, hits the floor next. Shawn is cute as a button, seventeen, and peels off that waltz.

"Not bad," Kym whispers.

"Not bad, my ass. I'm gonna have to bump her off."

Our turn. We hit it hard. I feel strong. We walk over to the three fake judges, who are all extremely complimentary and kind.

"David, you are so graceful."

"Your lines are beautiful."

"The command of the floor—really a wonderful surprise. I think you're in this competition to win it."

"Thank you, fake Len," I say. "Thank you, fake Bruno. Thank you, fake Carrie Ann."

We hustle backstage and get our fake scores from fake hosts.

"6 . . . 6 . . . 6."

"What?" I say. "Why such low scores?"

"It's fake, David," Kym says. "These are fake scores."

"But the fake judges were so nice to us before. They could've given us better fake scores."

"It's just the dress rehearsal," Kym says, dragging me away.

Doesn't bother me anyway.

Because we're good.

THE FIRST EPISODE

March 14, 2009.

Full disclosure. Right before the show I'm shaking like a leaf and I want to puke.

I am a nervous wreck. I am more anxious, more nauseous, more unsteady than I ever was before I appeared on Broadway. Even the first time on Broadway. I am afraid I will be sick and won't be able to go on. I imagine then that I'll have to take a drug test and we'll really be fucked. Somehow I get it together and make it down the runway without tripping or vomiting. Tom Bergeron and Samantha Harris, the hosts, introduce us—I wave and smile sickly—then introduce the judges, Carrie Ann Inaba, Len Goodman, and Bruno Tonioli, an Italian Simon Cowell wannabe. He's cast as the evil judge known for his wicked and nasty comments, which would be even more wicked and nasty if I could understand what the fuck he was saying.

As we start the show, I calm down. First of all, I've worked hard. In fact, I don't remember when I've ever worked harder.

Second, Kym is great. She's so great that she makes me look good.

And I know this. After putting in all this time and hard work, we're really dancing well. I think we're going to surprise those judges. In other words, we're good.

We do our dance and walk excitedly over to the judges.

Bruno, in his fractured English, says, "Some good lines. But you play four or five characters. Daveed, one character will suffice."

Carrie Ann adds, "Be careful with your face."

Len throws in for good measure, "David, your bottom sticks out."

As I'm listening to the judges, I think, *The producers have set me up! They've told the judges to focus on my face!*

What's worse is that I care.

I am not supposed to care. I am not supposed to take this seriously. This is supposed to be one big goof.

It's not. It's brutal. It is a competition.

We get our scores: 6, 7, 6. Mediocre. Less than we deserve. I suddenly feel small. I am wounded. Pissed off. I revert to fifth grade. I've just been kicked out of class and called before the principal.

I did not expect the judges' reaction, and I am shocked at mine.

Afterwards, backstage, Kym tries to calm me down.

"It's all right, David, we don't want to peak too early. These scores aren't terrible."

"We were better than that," I say.

"The judges were a bit harsh."

"Harsh? They reamed us! And what is all that crap about my face? What about our *dance*?"

"They were tough. Especially Bruno."

"Really? Bruno was hard on us? I didn't realize that BECAUSE I DIDN'T UNDERSTAND A WORD HE SAID!"

I start to storm off. Whirl around. Come right back at Kym.

"Next week is salsa, Kym. I am going to rip this salsa. You hear? Because salsa is in my blood."

She looks at me doubtfully.

"My first wife was Puerto Rican. I got ex–in-laws all up and through Manhattan. I know half the Puerto Ricans who live in every project in the Bronx, okay? I've got this dance down. Now, I never really learned how to *do* the salsa. My ex–in-laws told me that every time I saw them. But whatever. I have salsa in my blood, Kym. Hear? Well, okay. Kinda."

I storm off now for real.

I think I have made myself quite clear.

REHEARSAL, WEEK TWO

Last week ain't nothing compared to this. This week I work harder than I ever have in my professional life. It is 24/7 salsa. We go on You-Tube and find footage of the baddest vintage salsa ever. I'm talking about street salsa. Unlike the waltz, I pick this up fast. I lock this motherfucker down. And Kym and I are in synch, like a well-oiled machine. During our run-through, the cameraman actually applauds, says, "Guys, what I just saw there, that's a 10."

I beam, Kym giggles, rubs her hands through my hair. My hair crunches. It sounds as if I've sat on a large bag of potato chips. Kym backs away.

"Don't do that to my hair, honey," I say. "The whole thing may come off in your hand."

The camera is everywhere all week, following me like a stalker, filming every second. At one point, someone asks me how I felt when Bruno said that I played too many characters, made too many faces during the waltz.

"I really didn't understand Bruno," I say. "He needs subtitles. *Daveeed, you're having too many feces—*"

The crew laughs. Bruno, when he sees the footage, doesn't.

EPISODE TWO

March 16, 2009.

Salsa. I nail this motherfucker. Kym and I kill. From the first moment, I can tell in her face that we are cooking. When we finish, the audience goes nuts. Standing ovation. As we walk over to the judges, my legs are wobbly, from both excitement and exertion.

Bruno goes first.

"Daveed, it seems you don't understand me, so let me be very, very clear. Your timing was off—"

Then he starts deep-digging in my ass *again.*

Carrie Ann follows. Her comments are worse.

"Just because something is harder doesn't mean it's better. David, you were dancing on top of the music—"

I'm so shocked that I can't focus on anything else she says. In fact, I zone out completely. I hear only Len's very last comment: "That wasn't a good dance."

If Kym doesn't tug on my hand and pull me away from the judges, I'll still be standing frozen in front of them.

In the red room, Samantha Harris asks how I feel about the judges' comments. I summon up all my years of training, experience, and dealing with trials under stress and say, "I have two words for the judges. Hope and change. I hope we do better and that we can change their minds."

Kym laughs, nervously. I smile, holding back a world of pain, hurt, and anger.

Then the scores come in: Bruno: 6; Carrie Ann: 5; Len: 5. Total: 16. Terrible.

Microphone shoved in our faces. I'm blank. Fucking blank.

"How do you feel about the scores?" Samantha asks.

"We're in trouble," Kym says.

✳   ✳   ✳

We go to commercial. I hold it together until I hit the hallway, where I go absolutely, fucking primal.

"This show is fixed! It's rigged! The fix is in! I can't win! These motherfuckers!"

I then scream louder than I ever have in my adult life. My voice echoes off the motherfucking walls, slams back into my head, off the ceiling, up from the floor, and careens back like a thunderclap. I am a lunatic.

Of course, the camera is rolling.

"This is BULLSHIT!"

"David, what are your feelings tonight?"

"You want to know my exact feelings?"

"That would be lovely."

"My feelings are that these judges can suck my cock! They can eat a big veiny dick and suck MY ASS!"

I see Kym out of the corner of my eye. She rests her hand on my arm.

"David, shh, calm down. You have to calm down—"

"Calm down? You mean to tell me that I have to be judged by these motherfuckers? Twenty years in show business. Succeeded in every medium. And now I'm judged by some guy who wore a dance belt in an Elton John video in 1989, and Carrie Ann Inaba, who was a Fly Girl and showed her tits in a Madonna video? Fuck you! FUCK YOU! I CAN'T WIN! I. CANNOT. *WIN!!!*"

Now Kym is crying and the camera clicks off, and for one lost moment I consider walking off the show. Ending it right here. Right in this fucking hallway. I realize instantly that would be even worse. I can't walk off *Dancing with the Stars* because the judges were mean. How would that look?

I need to find my cool. I need to relax. Put this in perspective. There. Better.

"THOSE IGNORANT, LIMEY, BUTT-SUCKING, MOTHER-FUCKING, SHIT-EATING, COCKSUCKING *MOTHERFUCK-ERS!!!*"

Okay. I still might have a little way to go.

✴　✴　✴

The next day I walk into rehearsal determined to get it together. I ask Kym how bad things really are. She bursts into tears.

"Okay," I say. "You're the pro. From now on, I'm looking to you for leadership here."

"We have to get the judges back on our side," Kym manages between sobs.

"How's this? I won't spit on the ground anymore when I see them backstage."

Kym laughs. "That's a start. David, you're antagonizing them."

"I didn't say anything. I just stood there."

"That's antagonizing them," Kym says. "They have very big egos."

"They do?"

"Yes, David. You have to massage their egos."

"I have to massage their fucking egos? Who the fuck are they?"

Kym stares at me. "It's called *Dancing with the* Stars. They think they're the stars."

Damn. She's right. I finally get it.

"Okay. No more ghetto stares. No more eyeball fucking."

"Thank you."

"I will try to play along. You tell me what to do and I will do it. I'll be nice. I will maintain my composure. But if the judges keep fucking with me, this is gonna end badly. We will go down in flames."

"Just try."

"I will. It's about the team. There's no *I* in *team*, baby."

I smile and show Kym the new DAG. Dancing DAG.

But inside I'm barely holding it together.

I get home that night, limp into the bedroom. Christine is sleeping. I shake her shoulders.

"Wake up, Christine, wake up!"

"What are you doing? Be quiet. You'll wake the baby. What's the matter with you?"

"Christine, the judges hate me."

"What? What judges?"

"The judges. On the dancing show. They hate me. It's horrible. They're killing me. I don't know why they hate me, but they do. I'm working so hard. But it doesn't seem to matter what I do. I just can't please them."

A really long pause as Christine looks at me for an extremely long time.

"Okay, David, you have obviously lost your mind. I'm going back to sleep now."

But that is the turning point. That is the point at which I shift everything—my work ethic, my attitude, and, most of all, my will to win.

I want this bad.

✳   ✳   ✳

We're safe!

America votes, and Belinda Carlisle is the first to go. What's shocking is that Kym and I are voted among the top three. Teary good-byes to Belinda, the stage manager releases the audience, and a line of reporters forms to interview each couple. Each one asks me the same thing.

"What is going on?"

"What are you talking about?"

"With you and the judges. Clearly, they hate you."

"Really?"

"Oh, yeah. What is with Carrie Ann? Why is she so mean to you?"

"I don't know—"

"Do you have a history? Did something happen between you and now she's getting back?"

"No! Not at all."

"Well, the judges hate you. That's for sure."

"Where are you getting this? From the online message boards?"

"No. From the other dancers. They're all telling us."

"Holy crap," I say to myself. "I've got to turn this around."

That night, feeling pummeled, pissed, and disrespected—no, hated—by the judges, I pull into my driveway after the show. My neighbors across the street, three little girls, hang out of their bedroom window, waiting for me. Since it's a school night, their parents don't allow them to watch TV.

"David!" they shout.

I wave.

"Did you make it?"

My face cracks into a smile.

"I made it," I say.

They shriek and applaud, then close the window and scramble inside.

Well, the judges may hate me, but at least I have three loyal fans.

EPISODE THREE

March 23, 2009.

The fox-trot. I ratchet it up to redline. I practically kill myself rehearsing. Kym decides to focus the fox-trot on me. Her choreography is brilliant. This week my whole demeanor is different. I appear to accept the judges' "constructive criticism." I'm keeping my promise to Kym. I have morphed into the ultimate team player.

I say, "This is the hardest I've ever worked. We just have to keep going. I am working my booty off. I feel we're gonna bust out this week."

We do.

Bruno says, "Daveed, you've taken the fox-trot to Broadway! What a transformation! You are like Ben Vareen!"

Carrie Ann says, "Two snaps up, David! I didn't know you were a Rockette. Fantastic!"

Len says, "Best dance you've done, David. Bravo!"

Backstage we get our scores: three 8s. Tom Bergeron asks me, "So, David, what do you think of the judges this week?"

I break into an impromptu song, *"These are the greatest judges in the worrrrllddd."*

Tuesday night, after making us sweat by not calling our names until late in the show, we make the cut and say good-bye to Holly and her titties. In the press line afterward, I'm gracious and humble. I tell America that I'm thrilled that we've survived and that I just want to make Kym and my family proud. I drive home, feeling that I now have this game figured out. I pull into my driveway and climb out of the car. The three little neighbor girls are at the window, waiting.

"David, did you make it?"

I wave. "Yep. I made it."

They howl, hug each other. They've made my night.

Inside, I go online and check the message boards and blogs. Amazing. Everyone still says the judges hate us. Except for Kym's number-one fan. He says, "Kym Johnson deserves to win. Why? Because she is the best dancer ever to be on *DWTS*. She won the Australian *DWTS* once already, and came in second twice on *DWTS*, USA. She should have won last year but Warren Sapp wasn't a good enough dancer. She had a really good dancer with Joey Fatone but he was too fat to win. Now they stuck her with David Alan Grier??? It's not fair!"

At this point, a parade of online losers start jumping into the conversation. One writes: "Kym's #1 Fan, I'm gonna leave this chat room 'cause you are freaking me out."

Kym's #1 Fan answers, "Why? Because I'm the only real Kym Johnson fan? Fine, go. I will just stay in my own chat room and post by myself. You obviously don't love Kym Johnson like I do, anyway."

So touching.

EPISODE FOUR

March 30, 2009.

The Lindy Hop. Talk about a dance that falls right into my wheelhouse. First, black people invented the Lindy Hop, and we made it complicated on purpose. If you have not grown up with the Lindy

Hop, when you try to learn it, you may just screw yourself into the ground.

Second, my extra-octane supplements begin to kick in, big-time. Sweat pours off me as if I've just hauled a load of pig iron uphill. My kidneys feel like raisins and I'm pissing Jell-O. Doesn't matter. I'm stoked. From the moment Kym choreographs our Lindy Hop, I slide right in. Feel as if I'm home.

"We're going for it this week," I say into the camera. "Going to do some crazy riffs. I feel like this is going to be a turning point."

Then, to show the judges how cool I am and how I've changed, I recite a poem that I make up on the spot:

> *DAG is here to stay*
> *DAG is going to dance*
> *Until his hair turns gray.*

I grin. The crew laughs. Kym shakes her head, but she's happy.

*　*　*

We hit this Lindy Hop hard. We murder that motherfucker. At one point, Kym and I actually do matching cartwheels. The audience goes nuts. It's not often that you feel you've knocked something out of the park, but in this case, backed by the swell of applause and the audience leaping to their feet, I know we have hit a home run.

Len says, "Fun, full of energy. It's too bad you lost your timing in the middle. Not your best, but not your worst."

Bruno says, "Good, Daveed. I agree with Len. You did lose a little bit the timing in your feetwork."

If I think Len and Bruno fall short in their praise, Carrie Ann manages to compliment me and fuck me over at the same time.

"Wow," she says. "I thought that was great. And, David, you're not the youngest cookie in the bunch, right?"

I try not to show any emotion. I try to pretend that I appreciate their bullshit comments. I sincerely try. I'm practically biting my lip backstage as Samantha Harris rams her microphone into my face.

"I guess you won't be singing this week, right, DAG?"

No I *in* team, I say to myself. *Do not lose it. Remember your promise to Kym.*

"*I'm still happy, Samanthaaaaaa,*" I sing.

The scores come in: 7 . . . 7 . . . 8. A total of 22. Less than we deserve. At this stage we're competing with couples who are hitting 30 or close to it on a regular basis.

My heart sinks. I won't be surprised if I'm voted off this week.

* * *

Tuesday, March 31, 2009.

I hate Tuesdays. Tuesdays are now days of dread. America holds my fate in their cell phones or on the *Dancing with the Stars* website. I'm on edge. I stop to get gas on my way in to the studio. The guy filling up his tank ahead of me says, "Hey, how's it going?"

"How's it going? The judges hate me!"

The guy's back in his car before he fills his tank halfway.

Guess I'm a little on edge.

* * *

When I get to the studio, Kym greets me with a huge smile.

"We're safe," she says.

"Really? How do you know?"

"My mom called from Australia. Everyone's voting for us. Then my dance teacher called. All of his friends voted for us, too. We're good. We're solid."

This is not exactly inside information or scientific data, but for some reason, I buy it. I guess I'm just starving for good news.

During the day, I joke around with the other cast members and dancers. We've become a kind of family. It's crazy, but I find that I'm rooting for them at the same time that I want to win.

At one point, I find Lawrence Taylor off in a corner by himself. He is sitting motionless. I can't tell if he's sleeping or in some kind of trance. I don't want to disturb him, so I say, very quietly, very politely, "Hey, Lawrence, what's up?"

"What's up, DAG?"

"Hanging in, you know. Hate Tuesdays, man."

He just nods. Then he opens his eyes into slits and looks at me.

"I cannot be spoken to this way," he says.

"The judges?" I say.

He nods again and whispers so low that I have to lean in to hear him. "I'm doing everything I can not to beat the shit out of those motherfuckers."

"I hear you," I say.

"I'm trying so hard not to level that motherfucking desk they sit behind and smash those motherfuckers."

Visions of Lawrence Taylor—the most feared football player in history—blasting an opposing quarterback come into my head. I picture him charging the judges, shearing the wood desk in half, and burying his head in Bruno's midsection.

"I would love to see you do that," I say.

A slight smile forms on Lawrence's face. "Tuesdays, man."

"Hate 'em," I say.

I'm tempted to tell Bruno, Len, and Carrie Ann to make sure they call Lawrence "LT" before they give him his next scores.

He hates being called "LT."

Tuesday night's elimination show.

A mind fuck.

The hosts announce the first two couples who are safe. Not us. Then a musical number. Then they announce two more couples who've made it through. Not us. Another musical number. My palms are rivers of sweat. My legs are wobbly. My knees are clanking. The number finishes. Tom and Samantha announce the next two couples who are in. Not us.

Standing behind Kym, I whisper, "We're fucked."

"Well, let's just be happy for the work we did," she says.

"Really? You gonna flip just like that? I thought you said we were good, we were safe, all of Australia voted for us."

"We worked hard. I'm honored to have met you."

Holy shit! We're done! I cannot believe this! Whacked in week four doing the Lindy Hop? This is insane!

Then Samantha and Tom announce the bottom two couples and don't call our names. We have survived.

After the press line, where once again every reporter acknowledges that we have become this year's most hated couple by the judges—I'm cast as the Darth Vader of *Dancing with the Stars*—we go to a cast party. Two producers, both British, approach me.

"Sorry if we threw you off a bit there, David," the first one says. "We wanted to tell you, but it makes for such better television if your reactions are genuine and spontaneous."

"Yeah, great."

"Oh, minor thing," the second one says, swilling red wine. "The camera and microphone picked you up saying, 'We're fucked.' You should be mindful of that sort of thing for next week."

"And upcoming weeks," the first one adds, a little too quickly.

"Uh-huh," I say, "will do."

I sense at that moment that we really are fucked.

I spend the rest of the night hanging with the cast, feeling as if my days are numbered. Only one thing lifts my spirits.

The three little neighbor girls.

They are waiting for me, in their pajamas, hanging out the window.

"David, did you make it?"

"Yep, I made it," I say, waving.

They shriek, giggle, and give each other high fives.

✳   ✳   ✳

EPISODE FIVE

April 6, 2009.

The Viennese waltz.

I'm resigned. We're not going to win this competition. The judges hate us. We have to devise a new strategy, a new mind-set. Dance for fun, dance for ourselves. One thing's for sure. I'm not giving up.

Last week at the cast party, Harold Wheeler, the musical director of the show, legendary Broadway musical director and arranger, said to me at the bar, "David, this show changes lives. Trust me." From now on, I'm going to go for broke, be polite, respectful to the judges, not gonna clown around. Gonna take it one week at a time.

Kym decides to try something ambitious. We will do a Viennese waltz that actually tells a story. I'm excited to try it. We choose a perfect song: "I Put a Spell on You." As the camera follows us during rehearsal, I show how hard I'm working. And when I'm asked to comment, I say, "We want to be flawless this week. I'm trying to clear up any mistakes. I don't want my booty sticking out. We're just working extra hard."

We hit the dance. It flows. I actually feel more fluid doing the Viennese waltz than I have during any other dance. Kym and I keep eye contact throughout, keep focused on the story of the dance. When we finish, we fall into each other's arms, exhausted, knowing that we have done our best. The audience is with us. They applaud wildly. I can't help grinning. This dance may actually have been our best yet.

We step up to the judges. I take a deep breath. I lock my smile in place.

Len surprises me. "I love the story you told. I thought it was a very good performance."

I grin wider. Len liked it!

Then Carrie Ann crashes our boat.

"I think I figured out what's been bothering me. You two are not really in synch. You're disconnected. That's your problem. I think I finally put my finger on it."

I feel my smile melt away and my chin rise in defiance.

Then Bruno seals it.

"The spell worked . . . at times. But, Daveed, when you lifted your leg, you looked like a dog at a lamppost."

Okay. All bets are off. I eyeball-fuck Bruno. Kym squeezes my arm, tries to make eye contact. I avoid looking at her. She pinches me now. She knows I'm two seconds away from charging the desk and going Lawrence Taylor on these motherfuckers.

The scores don't matter. For the record, they are 8 . . . 7 . . . 7—a total of 22. I'm seething. It would be one thing if I were playing, not really trying, and if I sucked as a dancer, but I'm not playing, I am really trying, and I am a good dancer.

Oh, yeah. This is gonna end badly.

16

★ ★ ★ **16** ★ ★ ★

"THIS IS GONNA END BADLY"

I wouldn't have won, anyway. Because for tonight's show, they hit us with a surprise. No one sees it coming.

"Ladies and gentlemen, welcome once again to America's number one show—*Dancing with the Stars*! I'm Tom Bergeron!"

"And I'm Samantha Harris!"

Huge applause.

"Thank you," Tom says. "Well, as you know, this year we've had an unprecedented rash of injuries. Some dancers are known for their bumps and grinds. Unfortunately, our dancers are known for their breaks and wounds."

They hold for the laugh. It comes, cranked up to gut-splitting by the laugh machine.

Tom continues. "This week was no exception. Apple cofounder, our beloved Steve Wozniak, had a terrible accident while rehearsing the Lindy Hop. He screwed himself into the floor of his rehearsal studio. Sadly, Steve has withdrawn from the competition."

A long collective groan.

"We will all miss his winning smile and jocular personality. Thankfully we have found a suitable replacement. You've seen him on *60 Minutes,* as a frequent guest with Jay Leno, David Letterman, Jon Stewart, *The View,* and even on *The Factor* with Bill O'Reilly. Ladies and gentlemen, now dancing the Lindy Hop with his partner, Karina Smirnoff, please welcome to *Dancing with the Stars* the president of the United States, Barack Obama!"

Music swells and Barack Obama dances out of the wings, onto the dance floor, with Karina. He's dressed nattily, in a thin–pin-striped navy blue suit. Clearly, Karina has focused this dance on him, and within five seconds it's clear—

Our president can dance.

He's full of energy, he's light on his feet, he's slick; his steps and moves are crisp, clean, and sharp. He swings Karina around, between his legs, over his head. He's a veritable dance machine! Out of their collective minds with delirium, the spectators leap to their feet. He bows to them, bows to his partner.

He steps over to the judges and holds up his hand to quiet the crowd.

"Thank you. But before we get the judges' scores, let me just say a few words about my stimulus package and my vision for hope and change for all Americans—"

He talks about helping out those who have lost jobs, he talks about the insensitivity of CEOs taking big bonuses in this time of economic crisis, he talks about providing health care for those in need, and I realize that not only am I fucked but all the other contestants are fucked, too. He's got this competition locked up.

He finishes his stimulus spiel, takes a few questions from the audience, which includes John King from CNN and Brian Williams from NBC.

Then he turns to the judges.

"All right," he says. "I'm ready. Bruno, hit me."

"Meester President, may I call you Barack? Barack, that was lovely! So wild, so frantic, so perfect! Maybe the best Leendy Hoop I have ever seen. Bravo, Barack. 10!"

Wild applause.

"Thank you, Bruno. And I really appreciate your 10, because I didn't understand a word you said. 'Meester President, a lovely Leendy—'"

What? The president stole my joke? I can't believe this shit. The crowd roars. Bruno loses it, holds his chest with one hand and pounds the desk with the other one.

"Mr. President, that was totally awesome," Carrie Ann says, fanning herself with her number wand. "It's so awesome that you're here! And that Lindy? AWESOME! 10!"

"Well, I have an advantage," President Obama says. "The Lindy Hop was invented by my people."

Another huge laugh, followed by applause.

"That was my line," I say to Kym, who's swiping at the tears streaming down her face. "I was going to say that."

"Don't you just love him?" she says.

Last, Len, who applauds respectfully and says in his stuck-up English accent, "Bravo! It's such an honor to have you on our show. Your dance was spectacular, and your bottom did not stick out at all. 11!"

"Ha, ha. Thank you. It's an honor to be here."

"Wow, our first ever *11*," Tom says. "I don't think you have much competition here, Mr. President."

"Well, true. But maybe I can get David Alan Grier to help me with my bowling."

Oh, huge, HUGE laugh, forget about it.

"So, okay," President Obama says, looking over at the rest of us and rubbing his hands together as if he's about to crack open a safe, "who's gonna finish second?"

Trash talk. From the president of the United States.

I hear pounding at my door. I blink my eyes open. I'm in my trailer. I have dozed off.

"David!"

Kym.

"We're walking to the stage."

"I'm coming." I pull myself to my feet, ignore my cracking knees, aching back, throbbing hip, join Kym, and head toward the studio.

Tuesday.

Doomsday.

✳   ✳   ✳

April 7, 2009.

We stand on the stage, tiered on the staircase, bathed in red light, waiting to hear our fate. I feel like Sean Penn in *Dead Man Walking*.

Tom announces the first two couples who survive. I barely hear the names. I just hear him say, "Steve-O, you're safe," and I lean down to Kym and, having forgotten the producers' warning, once again say loud enough for America to hear, "We are fucked."

The camera cuts off me onto the featured musical act. They perform. I can barely focus. Finally, after an eternity, Tom declares two more couples safe. Now I start to get pissed.

Here we go, I say to myself. *I know what's about to happen. It's me and Lawrence Taylor. They're gonna make me dance in the motherfucking dance-off.*

Time stops. Feels like I'm standing here for a month. Then, at last, it happens. Tom Bergeron. The Voice of God.

"David and Kym, Lawrence and Edyta . . . you are the bottom two."

I fucking knew it.

"But," Tom says cheerfully, "perhaps by repeating your Viennese waltz in tonight's dance-off, you can improve last night's scores. We'll combine your best scores with the audience vote, and, who knows, you might survive."

Who knows?

Who knows, my ass.

They know.

Backstage, I bump into Lawrence, who's as pissed as I am.

"Look, if I'm going home, man, don't make me dance," Lawrence says. "Just let me go. Why the fuck do I gotta dance all over again?"

I shake my head. "It's like *Groundhog Day* for ballroom dancing. You take the worst dances and make everyone watch them twice."

I find an open lane in the hallway, and I pace. I'm trying to walk off my fury. Failing. Someone from makeup finds me, starts coming at me with powder and a soft pad. I whirl on her.

"Please, get the powder away from me. Please. I'm not in a good mood."

She backs away.

Yeah. They fucking know.

* * *

The next three minutes whip by as if on fast-forward. Kym and I repeat our Viennese waltz. I try my best, I really do, but I feel clunky, out of synch, off the beat. We step up to the judges, who all wear faces of sympathy and finality. I feel as if I'm facing a Roman tribunal. They give us compliments and better scores than last night, but beneath the desk, I can hear them sharpening their knives.

Lawrence and Edyta repeat their Viennese waltz. Lawrence is barely trying. He's lumbering, heavy footed. He looks like he's putting out a campfire. I can hear people laughing in the red room. Lawrence and Edyta pull up to the judges knowing that they've blown it. The judges are kind, deferential, and if I weren't both so paranoid and so sure, I would swear I see them winking. They hand Lawrence and Edyta lower scores than they give Kym and me, but I know it doesn't matter.

Moments later, after the annoyingly melodramatic *dum-dum-*

dum-dum music cue signals our send-off, Kym and I, vanquished, eliminated, say our good-byes to Tom and Samantha. I tell America that I just wanted to make Kym proud. Kym says she is very proud of me and that dancing with me has been great. The music for the end credits comes up prematurely, and the other dancers and cast members spill off the steps and surround us, enveloping us in a group hug.

I actually tear up. Kym's eyes fill up, too, and I could be crazy, but I catch a tear rolling down Lawrence Taylor's cheek as well. He sniffles, reaches over and whispers in my ear, "Congratulations. I'm still here, damn it."

Our final press line. Immediately following elimination. As in instantly.

Reporters from every conceivable media outlet swarm around us. I mutter a silent vow: *David, keep your cool. Go out with class. Deflect, deflect, deflect.*

I muddle through the first few questions. Take the party line. Not hard at first because this much is true:

"I love the cast and the dancers. We were like a family. We all supported each other. Everyone was absolutely terrific."

I follow this up with a line of clichés every eliminated contestant utters: "Did the best we could"; "Left everything we had on the dance floor"; "An amazing experience"; "Went down fighting."

The interviewer, someone I know from *TV Guide* online, confesses, "You know, David, my husband doesn't watch the show. But he watched it this time for you. We're big fans. We voted for you. As many times as we could. They close you out after a while."

I smile. "Thanks. My mother called me last week and told me that she voted for me. I said, 'Mom, you know you can vote more than once. It's not illegal.' She called me this week and told me that she voted twice. Thanks, Mom," I say into the camera.

"Is it frustrating that you can't go on?"

"It is," Kym says, at my side. "We felt like we had more dances in us."

"Oh, yeah," I say. "I was getting so close to revealing my chiseled swimmer's body. In fact, I was going to show everything, but we were denied. I was gonna do next week's dance butt nekked. Wearing just a dance belt. Give 'em the whole booty jiggle."

Kym laughs, only slightly horrified.

Then the interviewer makes a tactical mistake.

She asks The Question.

"David, what about the judges? Do you think they treated you fairly?"

Kym taps my forearm. Feels as if she's tapping out a warning in Morse code: *David, please don't go there. Take the high road.*

The high road? Why, of course.

"I have no love for the judges. Well, except Len. I didn't agree with him, but at least he gave us constructive comments every week. The other two? I have no respect for them. They're not qualified to be judges. It's hard to take shit week after week from people who aren't qualified and you don't respect. It gets to you. Right now, I'm trying to bring some class to a classless situation. So . . . the other two judges can kiss my ass. I want to say to them both, in all sincerity: 'Fuck you.'"

The *TV Guide* interviewer stares, not sure she's really heard what she thinks she's heard. Kym covers her face with both hands, desperately trying to make herself disappear.

I don't care anymore. I decide to go out with guns blazing. An interviewer from *Access Hollywood* materializes, and after spouting my well-worn clichés, I unleash.

"Carrie Ann and Bruno? I have never seen such inflated egos fueled by so little talent. I heard that Carrie Ann Inaba felt bad. Well, she can kiss my ass. I mean *all* of my ass. Matter of fact, she can wrap her lips around my booty hole. That's probably physically impossible, but she can try. You know what actually makes me feel the most proud? I am most proud that I didn't climb across that table and slap the shit out of every one of those judges. That's my proudest accomplishment."

Good thing I took the high road.

I'm done. I hug Kym, thank her, make all the appropriate good-byes and thank-yous. Feeling bruised, defeated, numb, and not at all vindicated despite going off publicly, I lower myself into my car and drive home. I drive slower than usual. It's strange, but this night hasn't sunk in yet. It's ridiculous. I've just been voted off *Dancing with the Stars,* a reality television show, meaningless really, when you consider everything else that's going on in the world.

And yet I feel loss. Profound loss. It's crazy.

I pull into my driveway and I climb out of my car. My biggest fans, the little girls across the street, are waiting for me. Their sweet, pink faces fill up their bedroom window.

"David, did you make it?"

A lump rises into my throat.

"No," I say, forcing a smile. "I didn't make it."

For a moment, they can't speak. Finally, one says, "We voted for you."

"We'd vote again if we could," the second one says.

"We still love you," the third one says.

Suddenly, my legs feel heavy, and a weight from nowhere clamps down onto my shoulders.

"Thanks, guys," I say. I wave and slump slowly into the house.

*　　*　　*

By morning, the shit has hit the fan.

Somali pirates hijack an American ship and take the captain hostage, but AOL chooses to show my face on its portal. Apparently "Black Man Goes Off" is bigger news than "Pirates Attack American Ship."

Before I'm even awake, my phone is ringing crazier than the phones at Obama election headquarters.

My friend Drew Frazier, a brother from Brooklyn, calls me in shock. "What the fuck did you do?"

"Huh?"

"You're front-page news."

"Oh, great."

"You are all over. You managed to knock Barack off the front page. Hey, between us, what was the deal with you and your dance partner?"

"Kym? We got along great. It was like a marriage except we didn't have sex. Come to think of it, it was exactly like my marriage."

My brother comes through on call waiting. I let Drew go and grab my brother's call. Geoffrey is a part-time drug counselor. He tells me that the crackheads he works with are saying, "Man, your brother's still doing *Chocolate News*. He refuses to be canceled."

My father e-mails me, doesn't mention the insanity on the internet. He is upset that I've been voted off the show.

"Am I out of line if I call it racism? Were the judges so harsh because you went to Yale and you're a well-spoken black man? Or do they just hate you for all of your achievements? Regardless, I love you anyway. I thought you were wonderful."

My mother, thankfully, doesn't own a computer.

Drew texts me back. "You've become an ABM. Will you ever work again?"

"I'm an angry black man?" I ask my phone.

Shawn Wayans calls. He's concerned. "Hey, DAG, what's up?"

"Hey, Shawn, what's up?"

"I heard about the *Dancing with the Stars* shit, man. Well, you know, unless you live on Mars, it's hard not to hear about it."

"Yeah. I know."

"I'm sorry about them cutting you loose. Keep your head up."

"Thanks, man. I will. Appreciate the call."

Now, I've been through divorce. Never got that call. My dog died, my show got canceled, my girlfriend fucked half of Hollywood. Never got that call. But *Dancing with the Stars* takes you out and—

"Hey, DAG, are you all right? That must've been rough. I'm here for you, man."

My manager calls. "DAG, you have to do damage control. Call Jimmy Kimmel. See if he'll put you on tonight."

"It's that bad?"

"We can get through this. With some luck. And lots of money."

"I did kind of freak out," I admit. "Talk about a turnaround. I started the show as Byron Allen and ended up as 50 Cent."

"We have to think this through, make sure we make the right moves. Cannot afford to trip up."

"Really? I'm gonna be taken out by telling off the judges on *Dancing with the Stars*? What about when Britney Spears had a complete meltdown? Half of the L.A. SWAT team, plus helicopters, had to bust into her house, strap her down, stark raving mad, to a gurney, and pull her out, and she's fine? Robert Downey Jr. snorted a pound of crack, broke into the house next door, and fell asleep butt naked with his neighbor's wife. He's gonna win an Oscar and I'm never gonna work again because I told the judges on *Dancing with the Stars* to kiss my ass? I'm fucking done because of that?"

"You have to chill."

"I swear the fix was in. That's the only explanation. Remember Master P on that show? He never took off his baseball cap, refused to wear dance shoes, could barely walk across the floor—and he lasted longer than I did! I'm the only person in history who's done *Dancing with the Stars* and come out worse than when I started."

I stop dead in my tracks. A moment of eerie calm, followed by a sudden spectacular flash of insight, hits me.

"Hold on. Is there a stand-up special in this? I think people may want to hear this fucked-up story."

"Now you're talking," my manager says. "That's how you turn lemons into lemonade. Add a fifth of vodka and you have something. I'm hanging up and making some calls."

In the end, after a few days, when I get some perspective, I realize that as hurt as I was at first, as disrespected by the judges, it all turned out the way it was meant to. Gilles, of course, wow. It would have taken a meteor to hit him for him to lose. Or they would've had to have found Gilles drunk in a gutter, saying, "America can kiss my ass," and his shit would have been over.

But when I left, Gilles and Cheryl were not taking any chances. Gilles and Cheryl brought in a shaman to come in regularly and cleanse their trailer. They wore special matching amulets that supposedly gave them secret powers. Really.

So what have we learned?

Number one: Consider therapy. Number two: Consider medication. Number three: Consider both.

And, number four, most of all, as much as I wanna be, I'm not really like Barack Obama.

The man has had every epithet thrown at him, been vilified, attacked, called every name in the book starting with "socialist" and then getting nasty, received more hate mail and death threats than any president in history, and still he remains unflappable, cool, calm, measured, controlled, confident, extremely presidential, and shockingly cheerful.

Barack like me?

I think not.

If Barack were like me, he wouldn't have made it past Iowa.

Can you imagine if Barack were like me during the 97 debates he had with Hillary? He would've gone ballistic within the first five minutes of the first debate, thrown up his hands, and said, "You are misrepresenting both my character and my polices. In other words, you can kiss my ass."

Fortunately, for the country, for the world, for every human being alive, Barack is not like me.

He'd never go off the way I did, even if he did go on *Dancing with the Stars* for real and the judges disrespected him. I think that show would send him over the edge way worse than dealing with the Republicans.

"I don't believe it, Anderson. President Obama has just leaped over the desk and has started to slap the judges."

Well, I can dream.

But at the end of the day, we know that Barack is not like me, thankfully, and I'm not like Barack, much as I wanna be.

And that's the story of my life.

ACKNOWLEDGMENTS

First and foremost, I would like to thank my parents, for nurturing, feeding, and fueling my sense of humor and intellect. Also thanks to my brother Geoffrey. Thanks to my agent, Kirby Kim. Thanks to my editor Sulay Hernandez, to Marcia Burch for being an early supporter, and the sales and marketing team at Simon & Schuster. And finally to Alan Eisenstock, without whom this book could not have been possible.

Printed in the United States
By Bookmasters